Wake Up World

A book by Martha Mansfield

BALBOA
PRESS

A DIVISION OF HAY HOUSE

Original front eyelid & back cover eye design by Phoebe Jacobs

Front eye ball design copyright of NASA:
http://www.nasa.gov/images/content/297755main_GPN-2001-000009_full.jpg

Main cover design by the Author with technical assistance from D.V.

Balboa Press books may be ordered through booksellers or by contacting:

Balboa Press
A Division of Hay House
1663 Liberty Drive
Bloomington, IN 47403
www.balboapress.com.au
1-(877) 407-4847

ISBN: 978-1-4525-0409-4 (sc)
ISBN: 978-1-4525-0410-0 (e)

Printed in the United States of America

Balboa Press rev. date: 05/02/2013

Special preface to the 2013 publication,

To my readers,

As 2013 dawns, so many issues are now seen in the light. I'm so grateful that as I've been working towards publication, this truth seeking is occurring in abundance! I want to emphasise, as I do in the Reading notes (which I recommend you read first), that although much has changed we are still dealing with the same core issues; how to create peace, not just globally but within ourselves, as it is this peace within and without that truly brings about the changes many of us want, both personally and globally.

I'm delighted Obama is in for a second term, as this continues to unite Americans across cultures and races and encourages greater voter input. As a human rights advocate I always want to see the middle to middle-left side of politics win over right-wing parties. Yet above and beyond, what this world needs from the voters of EACH country, is a willingness to *have their voices heard,* to advocate Always for fairer and more socially just policies; to work towards human rights legislation that is actually implemented; to demand practical support be given to those most desperate; not just within individual countries but locally, regionally, nationally, *and* Globally.

This book represents the thinking I felt many shared during the dark days of the Bush II U.S. administration, yet out of these years so much renewed activism was born; urging us to elect leaders who get this change in thinking, that we are not victims of our own governments, but as citizens are instruments through which fairer policies can be shaped. Organisations like the Get-Up campaign have been crucial in *proving* just how much power engaged citizens can have in influencing local, regional and national government policy.

In reviewing the wars in Iraq and Afghanistan, this book aims to give valid information which some readers may still not be apprised of. Some may feel they are 'over' hearing about this, but I attest that the citizens of the Coalition *can* not and *do* not 'get over' the reality of the suffering that is enforced, and certainly it isn't 'over' for the citizens we waged war against. It's always essential to understand the *whys* and that voters in the Coalition countries *can* advocate for true reconciliation and Healing with both these war torn countries.

I wish you all greater peace and happiness as we each realise the power in our own lives, voices and votes. I believe it is the responsibility of all who can to voice for justice for those who can't, as we wouldn't accept any less for ourselves.

Thank you for taking the time to purchase this book and please recommend this book to all those you think may find value in its messages.

Many Blessings and Thanks to All,
Martha Mansfield

'For Humanity'

CONTENTS

READING NOTES.. vi
INTRODUCTION... xiii

PART ONE – Wake Up World.............................1

    Chapter 1 – Humanity............................. 1
    Chapter 2 – Prejudice............................. 21
    Chapter 3 – Understanding....................... 48
    Chapter 4 – What can you do?....................... 54

PART TWO – The ways we deny our own humanity..63

    Chapter 5 – Lack of awareness.................….. 63
    Chapter 6 – Guilt................................... 68
    Chapter 7 – Distraction............................83
    Chapter 8 – Television.............................90
    Chapter 9 – Advertising.......................... 107
    Chapter 10 – Self-criticism...................... 120
    Chapter 11 – Self-abuse.......................... 123
    Chapter 12 – Choosing power over peace….. 132
    Chapter 13 – Violent computer games…….. 138
    Chapter 14 – Addictions in society…........ 149
    Chapter 15 – Pop music and sex selling....... 155
    Chapter 16 – Drugs and alcohol................ 164
    Chapter 17 – Depression......................…... 175
    Chapter 18 – Judgment and hypocrisy…….. 186
    Chapter 19 – More on society.................. 192
    Chapter 20 – Greed.............................…... 201

PART THREE – Where do we go from here?...........208

    Chapter 21 – Conscious awareness............ 208
    Chapter 22 – Global warming.................. 219

Chapter 23 – Creating the Universe...........225
Chapter 24 – The healing of the Human race
                    and Planet Earth...............235

END NOTES...245
REFERENCES...248
RESOURCES..251
IDEAS AND SOLUTIONS............................259

READING NOTES

Welcome reader!

This book covers some serious issues so I recommend reading the following points for clarification and context. It's essential to note the entirety of this book could be prefaced with the words: 'In my opinion'. This is an account of my own beliefs and my personal appeal on behalf of all those who are suffering:

- When I began writing *Wake Up World* in May 2005, I had no idea how much would change when it was finally edited in 2009. I therefore ask that you view the relevant matters in their historical context, however recent. The fundamental issues of humanity hold importance regardless of what year it is; some details may have changed but the core issues stay the same. I have thought at length about how to present this book post the Howard government in Australia, and years since I began writing. At that time, the sheer anger I felt over what was happening impelled this work into being. I believe the writing here is indicative of a growing sentiment felt by others who are seeing through the veil of what we call 'free democracies'. I began this book on the premise that many were still ignorant; conservatives remained in firm control, yet in the duration of writing people have been awakening at an exponential rate and this continues. To be true to its original design I have left its essentially fiery nature intact; I can only hope that such a dialogue holds value for future generations, let alone for this one.

Yes, many things are changing for the better. Much of what I have asked for in this book is actually manifesting and for this I am forever grateful. During these times of great positive change it is imperative that we stay involved and continue in this direction; staving off complacency as is necessary. The positive changes occurring do not change the truth of the immediate past; it is in fact this past which inspired us to change at all. So understanding this history is crucial. Informed and compassionate people of free societies become the driving force through which ultra-conservatism is ultimately rejected.

- Although this book contains criticisms against the George W. Bush administration[1] and the 'Coalition of the willing', please note that my thinking on this applies to all those in the world oppressing other human beings *wilfully* and *purposefully*. I focus chiefly on the Coalition as Australia is a member, and because the deceptions are only more insidious when it is the so-called 'leading democracies' of the world that are doing the destroying. This book is a stand against *all* inhumanity and my response to

---

[1] This government came to power dubiously in 2001 due to the U.S. Supreme Court's decision to grant Bush the presidency; this after a hotly disputed election where many thousands of voters were taken off the electoral role, mostly black citizens, whilst many other votes were recorded incorrectly or arbitrarily discounted. The Supreme Court's decision effectively denied the recounting of votes, which many have said would have made Al Gore president.

our acceptance of it. It is crucial to point out that when I refer to the U.S. as a country I am chiefly referring to the above said government and the people who supported them. There are many citizens and human rights activists in the U.S. that do not support inhumane policies; by realistically discussing the nature of U.S. foreign policy I in no way mean to refer to people who do not support this. I also do not wish to discount the positive traits of democratic nations; it is their wealth made at the expense of so many other nations that is of concern. In all conflicts there is damage caused to each side; I believe *all* parties must desist in violence or oppressive tactics if peace is to ever be achieved.

- This is by no means a scholarly thesis; this is one human's view. I have tried my utmost to present information as accurately as possible[2] but this is still my perception of that information. On all subjects I encourage you to seek your own truth in your own ways.

- The work of world renowned author Louise L Hay has had a strong influence on me, and if any writing in this book reflects that it is duly noted here. I developed my own understanding of spirituality prior to doing outside research

---

[2] Much of the information I have written on the Bush II U.S. government is backed up by the people who have been involved. You can see many of them speaking about their experiences directly through the documentaries listed in RESOURCES.

which upon finding (as is often the case) this new information resonated with what I already believed. I find Hay's writing is a particularly outstanding source of knowledge, and I cite her work accordingly.

- The information I share with you in this book is from sources that I have come across before or during writing; you may have come across similar information from different sources. There are many academics that have researched extensively and are doing a great deal of work in the area of human rights, developing excellent strategies to help create global equality which could lead to World Peace.[3] If you look at the work of academics and advocates of cosmopolitanism such as David Held and Daniele Archibugi you will see what I mean by this.[4] These are excellent sources for anyone who wants to review the policies that show how World Peace could actually be enacted; we are no longer living in the realms of wishful thinking.

- Special note to readers who may be sensitive to some issues: Part One of this book discusses human rights abuses and states the need for a compassionate response. There is information

---

[3] Please note: this is not referring to global communism! It is about bringing an end to the human rights abuses which are still prevalent throughout most of our world.

[4] These are academic writers I came across during a Masters of International Politics course I began whilst completing this book, as writing it inspired me to study farther.

regarding self-empowerment throughout the book so if you do not want to tackle the human rights issues now but are interested in self-health, I suggest you look up those subjects of interest and read the rest of the book at a later date if desired. Alternatively you can start from Part Two. Keep in mind that some chapters in this section may still be unsettling for some readers due to the language used; yet it's difficult to discuss those subjects realistically otherwise.

- I go into a lot of depth in my observations of current trends in Western culture (not limited to Western countries) and want the reader to know that in my discussion of violence and sex on TV (for example) I am not advocating that all violence and sex on TV should be banned; I am expressing the need for their to be *some* questioning, *some* morality; that some decent thought be given to these issues. If we do not comment on the extremism of what is being sold to us and how it is being sold to us regarding these subjects, these trends only grow more extreme.

- I use the term 'you' a lot and of course the context of this changes, depending on the subject. Perhaps those asleep will never read this, but I do refer to them nonetheless; their awakening is in fact crucial to us all. Many who once ignored these issues are in the process of opening their eyes to them. My use of the terms 'our' and 'we' may refer to people in Australia, the collective society of First World countries, or to all of humankind.

- When referring to a greater power or expressing great passion, I avoid using the term God as I do not want to affiliate myself with any particular religion. I have replaced most of these terms with ones that resonate with my true beliefs, such as The Universe, or All Atoms (see Chapter 24 for more on this subject).

- I am very glad to report that the Howard government has now been voted out, and that a calling of this book—even before it was printed—has been answered. This book explores the feelings *I* had during Howard's reign. It discusses the suffering I *know* that government inflicted upon many; the suffering that all right-wing governments ultimately bring. Unfortunately the damaging effects of the Howard government will linger long after it has left office. A Labour government does not equal there being a great increase in the standard of human rights, in this or any other country, but it is certainly a step in the right (left[5]) direction. Voting Liberal—post the Howard government—is still voting for war, the division of rich and poor, racism, discrimination and ultimately, inhumaneness. Let's pray Labour bring us back to some saneness and humaneness.

---

[5] When I refer to left or left-wing, it's important to note that what is labelled 'extreme left-wing' is communism; in most cases this type of government has amounted to dictators controlling the masses and therefore little different to fascism (extreme right-wing). I believe somewhere between the middle and left (such as could be achieved with deliberative democracy) is about the right balance.

- At the end of some chapters I have added farther Ideas and Solutions. You can read these in entirety at the end of the book.

- M.M. stands for Martha Mansfield.

   Thankyou and Enjoy!

INTRODUCTION

If we keep our eyes closed for long enough, by the time we open them, there may not be a world left to see. M.M.

Dear Reader,

It is becoming increasingly clear—only because people are starting to listen and the evidence is incontrovertible—that the environmental damage caused since the Industrial Revolution is having dire consequences on our planet. This is such a serious issue that human consciousness is the only hope we have of saving our Planet Earth. Those that make billions off the coal industry must fund sustainable and safe energy alternatives. Australia was a world leader in solar technology before Howard sacked our experts on renewable energy, as well as starving the industry of funding, soon after he became Prime Minister.

We now have over 6 billion people living on earth where we had around 1 billion at the beginning of the last century. That's a *hugely* accelerated growth. But what education and resources are available to those who are populating at a massive rate? None; many are starving and exploited.

It is my honest belief that the destruction inflicted upon human beings is just as crucial an issue as the destruction inflicted on the planet. In fact, how can we separate the two problems and say that one is more or less important than the other? We *are* our environment; a single species out of up to 30 million, most of which are declining rapidly. Many would say that the issue of human rights abuses should take priority over the earth, as we don't technically know if it feels pain due to our actions but we *do* know how devastating human rights abuses are for those who suffer them; still, both these problems need to be solved if we are to live in a healthy and sane world.

This is my argument for our species:

We are at a point in history where we now know, without a doubt, that there are many atrocities occurring throughout the world. And if we choose to sit down for our evening meal without ever discussing or thinking deeply about this, and most especially if we choose to vote in leaders that assist in these atrocities, then we have blood on our hands too.[6] This cannot be denied. 'They' (governments, power wielders, etc.) are relying on the fact that no matter what they do, the West, and all those living comfortably will continue along as if we really did live in a peaceful world where the rules of humanity are upheld.

Well, we know for a fact that this isn't true. We know those in power require our apathy to fulfil their frightful intentions. They are shaping the world in the way they see fit, and upholding human rights is certainly not on their agenda.

I am not saying that one is a bad person if they live their life in peace. I am saying that we each have a

---

[6] This statement in particular refers to those who actively support or deliberately ignore human rights abuses when they could make a small contribution to help those who are suffering, and not to those who for any reason are not able to contribute at this time.

responsibility to care about our fellow humans too. Who is to fight for their rights if not you and me? And all those free to live democratically? The masses must wake up!! We, as a country, are supporting human rights abuses overseas that we would never want to happen here, even though some do. This hypocrisy is a cross bearing down on our souls. To completely ignore the plight of others—hundreds of millions collectively—says to me that we may as well not be human, or enjoy the love in our hearts, for if we will not use those hearts for the purposes of good, and healing, and empathy, then really what's the point of having them?

What we wish for ourselves as single human beings, we must also wish for *all* beings. This is what humanity means. We *all* need the same things; air, water, food, shelter, love.

As the world has become global, so now we must begin to act as global beings. There are more opportunities for the world to unite over these issues than there has ever been before; as they affect us all.

I know many of you out there are doing what you can and as a fellow human I *deeply thank you* for all your work: nurses, teachers, healers, aid workers, environmentalists, counsellors, activists, people who care, artists who care, and to the journalists who risk their lives to show us what is happening, and thanks to all those who support these professions. M.M.

PART ONE – Wake Up World

Chapter 1 – Humanity

We are all born humanitarians, but it gets slowly but surely crushed out of us. For those of us that remember, it is time to re-activate it in others, for if we truly cease to care about humanity and human beings, we truly cease to be. M.M.

Wake Up World! If we let the fascists win—and they are winning in their part of the world where human rights abuses are accepted—the world we live in is ultimately affected. Living with fascism is not a world any human would choose to live in, but so many are living with oppression today. Even in Australia, we have experienced Howard's fascist leanings; tentacles entwining society, choking the rights of workers, families, people with disabilities, single mothers and all others not in big business. We are turning back the clock and it has got to stop! Howard has full control of the senate and is pushing laws through left, right and centre. And remember, he is mates with the guy who said: "If this were a dictatorship, it'd be a heck of a lot easier, just so long as I'm the dictator."[7]

But is that ok, if the Howard legislation benefits your situation? Is it ok to support the war because you got a $600 baby bonus?[8]

---

[7] George W. Bush as quoted at:
www.politicalhumor.about.com/od/bushquotes/Bushisms
This is one of many cited quotes. Accessed on February 12th 2006.

[8] The money given per baby born has since increased. This is not just a bribe for the middle class, but also an invitation to poorer women and couples. This is just one example of how

Is it ok to support policies that make the rich richer? And that might be helping you?

That is the micro level. The macro level is:

Is it right to live a life of luxury whilst masses of the human race are forced to suffer from starvation, terror and helplessness?

Can we really live out our lives ignoring the widespread violation of human rights, rights that apply universally, including to you and me?

Do we understand that corporations exploit people who are forced to accept base wages or starve to death?[9] It's time to start relating to all the 'goods' we buy that are 'Made in China' as the products of misery and oppression of real human beings.

Can we honestly sleep at night knowing that the pain inflicted upon others could just as easily be inflicted upon you or me if we were born into those circumstances?

Does it make the fascists right, because we are living comfortably?

I don't think so.

---

policy can be used to influence votes; the reality is if Howard supported paid maternity leave many mothers would be in a better position than they are with a one-off bonus.

[9] M Achbar, J Bakan, J Abbott, *The Corporation,* documentary, Big Picture Media Corporation MMIII, USA, 2004.

The whole point of humanity is that it applies to *every* human being, not just to those who live in the 'safe' or 'democratic' countries. This is a fundamental truth!

Human rights apply to all of us; those of us who do exist, those of us who have existed and those of us who will exist. It applies to all of us who are human. It's that simple.

But can you imagine if, in regards to the Iraq war, the shoe was on the other foot? Would you really want the tanks outside *your* door? What if the U.S. thought Al Qaeda was training here, say, in the desert? Would they have invaded Australia? Well, what if you lived in Iraq? Do you get that it is not that different there? There are *human beings* existing there, just as you exist here. There are people trying to earn a living, to feed and shelter their families, just like you.

Would you want sanctions on your country so that you cannot trade, or be supplied with essentials, like water and food? The Iraqis have had sanctions imposed by the U.S. (and allies) since the Gulf War (1990-91).

Noam Chomsky, a powerful intellectual, details explicitly the true nature of U.S. foreign policy throughout the world in his heavily documented work *Hegemony or survival*. In relation to the Gulf War, he states that:

> The 1991 war, involving the purposeful destruction of water, power, and sewerage systems, took a terrible toll, and the sanctions regime imposed by the US and UK drove the country to the level of bare

survival.[10] As one illustration, UNICEF's *2003 Report on the State of the World's Children* states that "Iraq's regression over the past decade is by far the most severe of the 193 countries surveyed," with the child death rate, "the best single indicator of child welfare," increasing from 50 to 133 per 1,000 live births, placing Iraq below every country outside Africa apart from Cambodia and Afghanistan.[11]

Many of you out there may not know to what extreme lengths the U.S. will go to farther its own interests in countries throughout the world.

> The US blocked water tankers from reaching Iraq on grounds so spurious that they were rejected by the UN arms experts, "this during a time when the major cause of child deaths was lack of access to clean drinking water, and when the country was in the midst of a drought."[12]

When you punish a leader for violating human rights it only punishes the masses of people under that regime. Whatever the reasons were, it wasn't Saddam that destroyed the water systems and prevented access to water which caused the deaths of hundreds of thousands of children in Iraq; it was the U.S. and allies.

---

[10] N Chomsky, *Hegemony or survival,* Allen & Unwin, Australia & New Zealand, 2003. Published in arrangement with Henry Holt and company, LLC, USA, 2003, p. 126. Chomsky adds in his end notes that these sanctions were technically imposed by the UN, but enforced by the US/UK, p. 254.
[11] Chomsky, p. 126.
[12] Chomsky, p. 128. The in-text quote is from academic researcher Joy Gordon.

One of the main selling points for the latest Iraq invasion was that Saddam was a 'bad man' (I am in no way here trying to dispute his past tyranny), but if this was the real reason for going to war, why the hell did the U.S. put him into power in the first place? Why did they sell him chemical, biological and nuclear weapons and support his regime when it suited them? Did you know that Saddam's rule was secular (i.e. non-religious), women were educated and Iraq was home to some of the Middle East's finest universities? "Horrifying and brutal as Saddam Hussein's regime was, he nevertheless did direct oil profits to internal development."[13] In most of the documentaries I have seen on the subject, many Iraqi people feel things are now much worse; at least under Saddam they had a modicum of security, freedom, and employment. Now most of the country is in the throes of destruction.

Perhaps some people believe that it is justifiable to invade Afghanistan and Iraq because the people there were oppressed under the previous regime, in this case, the Taliban in Afghanistan[14] and Saddam in Iraq. But if the U.S. were genuine in these matters, why not intervene in other oppressive regimes, like the Jundaweed in Sudan, the Burmese military or the Chinese government? Just to mention three. They are committing equally as horrific atrocities—and all atrocities are horrific—but no intervention there.

Interventions are problematic if those intervening have their own personal agenda. The case for "preventive

---

[13] Chomsky, p. 126.
[14] The U.S. was not even interested in Taliban atrocities; they were there for Al-Qaeda (among other things).

war" is a very dubious one, where "military force" is used to "eliminate an imagined or invented threat ... Preventive war falls within the category of war crimes."[15] Not dissimilar to preventive war, going to war in the name of humanitarian intervention is often used by those in power as an excuse to exploit a country already greatly suffering.

Isn't it obvious that the U.S. only invades countries where they have something to gain—oil, control, money? As well as ignoring the human rights abuses of countries they want to do business with, like Africa and China? They 'liberate' (bomb the hell out of) places for *personal gain,* in the name of 'democracy' and 'freedom', and we are even asked to praise them for their 'humanitarian interventions'! "As always, the US leadership can confidently take credit for the overthrow of the tyrants it supported until the very end."[16]

Imagine the difference a *genuine* intervention could make in Darfur, and other such places in turmoil? For to uphold human rights it is imperative to depose dictators and fascist regimes around the world and to erect moderate governments that will not cause harm to the people of that country. But how to do it?

By providing the essentials to people that desperately need them, while dealing with those in power who oppress them. For now, it seems, this would still require the use of force, because you can't fight guns with flowers. We need a weapon free world, and must learn to negotiate without violence, yet to stand by whilst

---

[15] Chomsky, p. 12.
[16] Chomsky, p. 114.

great violence is exerted upon those who are helpless seems incredibly heartless if there is a way it can be stopped. But the liberation of those who are oppressed can only be achieved if the intentions of the liberators are pure, where the needs of the people are actually considered and integral to the process.

But in America's case their intentions are anything but. Therefore tragedy and disaster ensue. If you look at the last 50 odd years, you will know that the U.S. *has* supported, and *does* support, hardline governments across the globe, continually employing oppressive tactics in many countries, and South America is no exception. The U.S. government has trained dictators, not to mention Bin Laden himself.

The U.S. *supported* Bin Laden and the Mujaheddin[17] in Afghanistan to fight the invading Russians in the 1980s, training many of the jihadis which they now call enemies. Afghanistan has an extensive and long history of power struggles and over thousands of years has developed a rich and complex culture. There is much rivalry amongst the many warlords and within the Mujaheddin itself. But *civil* war only broke out in Afghanistan after the U.S. withdrew their support, once their own objectives had been achieved. "After the Russians withdrew, the terror organizations recruited, armed, and trained by the US and its allies (among them Al Qaeda and similar jihadis) turned their attention

---

[17] Mujaheddin is an Afghan term meaning: "Holy warriors fighting jihad or holy war." (See Ahmed Rashid's *Taliban,* p. 245.) This was the group from which the Taliban emerged in 1994.

elsewhere ... "[18]

Just imagine what that country needed after a decade of war.

Ahmed Rashid, a journalist of 30 years and author of *Taliban,* has spent a lot of time in Afghanistan, and he observes: "The long years of US and Western neglect have allowed the Taliban to turn Afghanistan into just such a sanctuary for extremist groups ... "[19]

It is an absolute joke for the U.S. and the Coalition to say that they are 'fighting against terrorism' when through their own actions or inactions they have created fertile ground for it to occur. The U.S. provides weapons for Pakistan, who supported the Taliban! Post 9/11 Pakistan joined the 'war on terror' but their own backyard still serves as a training ground for many terrorist groups. Pakistan's commitment is hence 'in name only'. The Taliban continue to commit many barbaric acts against their fellow Muslims.[20] In 2001, Afghanistan was rated the worst humanitarian disaster zone in the world, with up to 5 million refugees.[21]

And this was before we invaded!!

The U.S. has major priorities in Afghanistan. Did I forget to mention that Afghanistan has some of the largest gas reserves in the world? Or that while the oil

---

[18] Chomsky, p. 111.

[19] A Rashid, *Taliban,* Pan McMillan Ltd, London, 2001, p. viii.

[20] Rashid, pp. 17-66.

[21] Rashid, p. xi.

fields of Iraq were being secured by American troops, the museum holding the world's records of our known civilization was left unguarded and consequently looted? And in taking control of the world's oil, the U.S maintains its control over the world.

According to Chomsky, the strategies invoked by U.S. foreign policy are ultimately borne out of an application of Wilsonian[22] ideology, particularly by the Reagan-Bush I and Bush II administrations; its implementation inflicting their own brand of terror upon many defenceless countries, and opening the door for many allied countries to do the same. They have a plan and there is a heavy price to pay. Just don't be fooled by all the peace talks. Start to understand them as war plans. It's your future too.

George Orwell, in writing about the Spanish Revolution, borne from the people's revolt against the dictator Franco, wrote this statement in *Homage to Catalonia*. I believe it holds relevance in situations where a government uses its power against the will of the people or when any government starts leaning towards fascism.

> Everyone, however unwillingly, took sides sooner or later. For even if one cared nothing for the political parties and their conflicting 'lines', it was too obvious that one's own destiny was involved.[23]

---

[22] The term Wilsonian refers to past U.S. president Wilson Woodrow. For more details regarding Wilsonian ideology, see Chomsky's *Hegemony or survival*. I highly recommend this book to anyone who wants extensive information about U.S. foreign policy.

[23] G Orwell, *Homage to Catalonia,* Penguin Books, England,

We must realise that as individuals the choices we make down at the polling booths affect all our futures. Don't choose that which you yourself could not accept.

****

Now back to Australia. I know John Howard has not been publicly accused of murdering masses of people—although in supporting the wars in Iraq and Afghanistan he has, through participation, clocked up *hundreds of thousands*—but he *has* locked away genuine refugees in grossly below standard conditions, some likening Australia's detention centres to the concentration camps run under Hitler. Now if someone makes a reference like that it best be taken seriously. Because even if those reports were grossly incorrect (they weren't), a fraction of the conditions of a concentration camp is extremely bad. Locking children up for years—no one can say those children were a threat to the community—watching their mothers and fathers and adults cut themselves in utter desperation, total isolation and suffering under great mistreatment.

One of the many 'scores' of the Howard government.

Nothing anyone can do or say can ever justify the indefinite and unlawful detention of a child, let alone any human being.

How does Howard sleep at night?

1962, p. 47.

With his fascist mind that 'accepts' (using *doublethink*[24]) the fact that he brutalises other human beings, convincing himself that they 'aren't really human' as if he had any comprehension of real human suffering there is no way he could allow such things to happen, much less make it law. He cannot comprehend the pain that is caused when certain actions are taken against people. He refuses to understand that human suffering is *real* and it is *felt,* causing pain some may never get over. When one is in extreme circumstances the only place one wants to be is anywhere but there, and to some even suicide may seem the only way out.

Can you imagine being locked up with no idea about your future, waiting for years while your case is 'assessed'? We still have many asylum seekers, including children, locked up right now! And those granted temporary visas have no access to resources like employment, education and welfare. They are forced into jobs with little pay and no rights and are barely surviving with the support of agencies such as the Asylum Seeker Resource Centre. Please remember that most, if not all of these people were *forced* to abandon their homes and would never leave their ancestral country by choice; would you?

I thought human beings were meant to be intelligent, but at that we are failing seriously. Because how long does it really take to assess a person fleeing from war or

---

[24] G Orwell, *1984,* Penguin Books, England, 1954, p. 223. Orwell explains: "*Doublethink* means the power of holding two contradictory beliefs in one's mind simultaneously, and accepting both of them."

extreme circumstances a refugee? They have no weapons, no money; they have nothing—literally! What harm could they really do? Do you understand that these people fled *from* harm; they are searching for a way to not *be* harmed, anymore, not the other way around! But how we treat these people when they arrive (if they don't die trying) is unspeakable. Get their names, id 'em, help them set up a little community with assistance from people who know what they're doing. The tax dollars of what all that will cost is a lot less than for a bunch of big massive prisons.[25] If these people can work, they'll work, even if that work only serves to sustain themselves and their community. It is not that hard for people to work together towards a common goal. Like survival. People do it all the time. There is no way any of those boat people had to suffer any more than what they already had, from what they were fleeing from. No need at all. Please note that while 4000+ boat people have sought asylum on our shores in recent times, other countries in the world have accepted *millions* of refugees. I hope you can see how utterly shameful and pathetic Australia's response has been.

At May 2007 there are over 4 million Iraqi citizens who have been displaced because of the war.

That's almost a quarter of Australia's population.

---

[25] Sadly, where detention camps are set up in Australia, a 'selling point' is the business it makes for the local communities, i.e. through employment, food services used etc. Yet there are many other ways to enrich communities that don't involve locking people up without charge.

As I've said, Howard cannot comprehend human suffering because *if he could,* there is no way he could implement his fascist policies. No way known. Would you lock away a neighbours kid, in a cage in the middle of the desert, because their parents tried to come to your house as theirs was been invaded? Or would you invite them in for a nice cup of tea, and try to sooth those who are obviously in a high state of terror and distress?

"What language do you cry in?"[26]

And think about how many asylum seekers have sought and will seek Australian shores that are fleeing the wars in Iraq and Afghanistan; wars we actively support. The inhumanity of this country's decision makers and their voting constituents in relation to asylum seeker policy is incomprehensible.

Human rights do not change on the basis of skin colour, age, sex, religion, race, and so on. It applies to all of those who are human. You or I cannot judge whether or not those asylum seekers are sincere. No one has the right to assume that any asylum seeker entering this country is a terrorist, and locking him or her up in case they are. Let's face it, the so-called terrorists that we know of are well-educated and rich, and often trained by America themselves! They are not spending their life savings on a one-way ticket through treacherous waters on a matchstick boat just to commit a terrorist act on whichever country they end up at. I mean, really. Spending your life savings does not make you rich as I've heard some people suggest boat people are; it

---

[26] Michael Franti & Spearhead, *Is Love Enough?,* music album, Yell Fire!, Michael Franti, Boo Boo Wax, 2006.

makes you desperate, it's a last resort. It's outrageous to say that any of the boat people are terrorists; utterly outrageous and practically impossible.

And in relation to terror, the war on terror *is* the terror. *"The war for oil is a war for the beast, the war on terror is a war on peace."*[27] It was Al Qaeda who claimed to be the perpetrators of 9/11. That's *one* terrorist group only and the attackers were mostly made up of Saudi Arabians who had defected, not Iraqis![28] Many of the so-called 'terror groups' that are added to the 'terror list' are people fighting for their very right to live in peace. These groups were created because *of* oppression, they are fighting *for* freedom. But now the Coalition (as did Reagan's 1980s war on terror) labels any oppressed group in countries allied with America a 'terror group', yet the Coalition has killed and will continue to kill hundreds of thousands more in the war on terror, than the terrorists ever could.

> Too many innocent people are dying in Iraq. A recent report, in the medical journal, *The Lancet,* estimates 100 000 Iraqi civilians have been killed

---

[27] Michael Franti & Spearhead, *Light Up Ya Lighter,* 2006.

[28] Please note that the Bush II U.S. government *did* have something to gain from the 9/11 attacks; they have used the loss of a few thousand American lives (although clearly tragic) to justify the invasion of two entire countries full of *tens of millions of people!* Why would a fundamentalist Muslim commit an act of terror that they *knew* would instigate wars in their homelands? There may be a lot more to this story than we have been told; either way the brutality of the U.S. retaliation and the many innocent lives that has destroyed is a great hypocrisy and I believe also disrespectful to the 9/11 victims.

since the beginning of the U.S. invasion. Half of them are women and children. Almost all were killed by Coalition air strikes.[29]

I quote this from an article printed in *The Age* on the 9th of November 2004. This amount is over 30 times the amount of those killed in 9/11. And as you know, many hundreds of thousands more have perished since.

I am not saying that killing innocents[30] can ever be justified, but it is of extreme importance to look at the motives. Look at the history of 1st World countries such as England and America. They have tended to invade and conquer countries, 'killing many innocents', for resources, profit, land, $$$s. (Hell, it's the English that invaded and colonised America and Australia in the first place!) Now 'terrorists' or 'enemies of the invader' or 'freedom fighters' of oppressive regimes seem to do the same thing, 'killing innocents' in the name of their cause, but their reasons are to fight the invasion of that extremely weapon rich country! Think of the cases of the U.S. invading Iraq, and Israel's occupation of Palestine. We are talking about the difference between armies that have hundreds of thousands of troops, with superior air power, weaponry and technology (the U.S. and Israel), versus a defenceless and dismantled Iraq, and Palestine with no army, and a police force of only 1200 odd members, with even fewer weapons! In cases

---

[29] A Waleed, 'How many innocent Iraqis is too many?' *The Age,* 9 November 2004.
[30] I use the term 'innocents' here but I could just as easily exchange it for 'people'. Soldiers killing soldiers is equally as undesirable. I don't believe in any form of killing except, perhaps, in extreme cases concerning self-preservation or for the protection of those who are helpless.

like these the death toll is always far, far greater, more than a hundred fold, for those who do not have the ability or resources to defend themselves. Killing innocents can never be justified, but if you think about it, retaliation *against* attack seems much easier to comprehend than outright instigation, occupation and invasion.

The most terrible thing is that when you do invade countries with the audacity that America has, you only provoke extremism, most especially in the young. *More than half of Iraq's population are under the age of 15.* And even those adults who were previously moderate may become radicalised once they have lost loved ones. People may then fall to extremism to seek revenge, or to gain control for their own reasons, and then wield power for their own reasons. Some people may even forget the freedom they are fighting for and instead become enemies of their own people. But is their thirst for power borne from the history of colonisation in those countries or is gaining power the only way they can survive? What do *you* think? People do not retaliate when there is nothing to retaliate against. America has invaded Iraq and Afghanistan and made no serious attempt to provide security to the people at large. And when you lose the rule of law, all hell breaks loose, and you are left with a broken society that slips into civil war. Please do not kid yourself that America did not only know this would occur all along; it was, in fact, desirable. Just look at who profits: the investors; the contractors; the business owners (not to mention those with shares on the stock market in all war-profitable corporations—*and there are plenty*); the soulless men that go there to 'rebuild' and build in that country. They bomb the town, kill many people, destroy their infrastructure, destroy their lives, and then start their projects, for their American companies. (Weapons of war have to be paid for—the lines between the Bush II administration and the companies that profit from arms manufacturing are blurred at best.) How I loathe every contractor who has gone and made millions and billions or *anything* in Iraq, while the country itself goes hungry. America had only spent 2% of the aid package designated for the protection of civilians to be used *immediately* after the initial invasion by June 22nd 2004, long after 'victory' had been declared. "Of 3.2 billion earmarked for security and law enforcement, only 194 million has been spent."[31] Doesn't this fact alone show you where their interests lie?

Meanwhile Iraq collapses into civil war. The devastating effect this is having on the Iraqi people was predicted by many before the U.S. invasion, and the story in Afghanistan is not much different.

Here is a succinct question posed by Michael Moore to whom he calls George Bush Jnr in *Stupid White Men* on that situation:

> As soon as your campaign to take control of Afghanistan was complete, you installed a former oil company consultant as the "interim leader." You then appointed a former Unocal consultant as our new ambassador to Afghanistan. Within a few months, a new deal was signed to build that pipeline across Afghanistan. Now that you've got what you

---

[31] R Chandrasekaran, 'US spent only 2% of its aid package', *The Age,* 5 July 2004.

want, can the troops come home?[32]

With no one to look after their greater interests, both Afghans and Iraqis continue to suffer in unimaginable ways, as we continue to moan about the price of petrol, yet in Iraq they pay up to $10 a litre for petrol and people must wait in long queues to acquire it! Can you imagine that happening in Australia? But where do we get our oil from?

Among the terrible irony of these wars is that they are only fuelling more wars, only fuelling terrorism. No matter how many 'terrorists' the U.S. capture or kill, they are only creating more enemies, due to their own oppressive tactics. You cannot win a battle when you are the burning fuel that emblazons it. Clearly, you can't 'save' a country when you are exploiting it for your own profit. Terrorists are the sorts of people that detain other people illegally and strip them of their human rights. Terrorists also bomb innocent civilians in the name of their cause. 'Operation Iraqi Freedom' should be called what it is: 'Operation Iraqi Destruction'. WE are the terrorists, the Coalition and the Australian government, a billion times over what even one of those boat people could have been.

Ideas and Solutions:

- Vote Howard out.
- Do not judge what you do not understand. Develop your understanding.

---

[32] M Moore, *Stupid White Men,* Regan Books/HarperCollins Publishers Inc., United States, 2001, p. 259.

- Fight for human rights in every way you can; talk to people!
- Watch documentaries, read books, seek the truth for yourself; mine is only one view.
- Whatever your opinion of Michael Moore, he does reveal the links between oil in the Middle East and the U.S. administration well in *Fahrenheit 9/11*.
- Analyse the polls; ask about second preference votes and where they go. Do not vote Family First, they are a fundamentalist Christian group which ultimately represses freedom. Labour have been supporting many of Howard's policies (and are closer to centre-right due to Howard's extremism), so unless they improve, the only decent option is the Greens. A Greens government would at least show the world we are committed to Peace and the Planet, rather than war and money. However, we need Labour in government until there are enough Green seats for the majority parties to be Labour and the Greens.
- Join any human rights activist groups that you can.
- The only reason the Howard government has managed to produce low unemployment figures is because Howard has created new laws forcing welfare recipients to work (for nix or as little as $30 a fortnight) to retain their welfare payment. Even 1 hour of unpaid work counts as employment which is why the 'work for the dole' scheme has been so effective in raising employment figures. Similarly our economy is only 'booming' because the rich are making a lot of money (and of course there are all those

mining exports to China) while the poor are getting ripped off even more.

- Just remember, you have been given this incredible gift of life, and it can never be justified that we have this at the expense of those who are being deprived of their gift of life. To truly appreciate what we have, we need to start working on this incredible inequality *now*.

Chapter 2 – Prejudice

"It would be much more constructive if people tried to understand their supposed enemies."[33]

I write this after the first of the terrorist raids in Melbourne and Sydney on November 8th 2005.

Do you have any idea how insane it is, that here I am, a white person, living on a white street, enjoying all the luxuries of a good home, enough food to eat, safety, heating, electricity, security, a way to make money, plenty of fresh water (for now), the right to democracy and freedom of speech, etc., whilst Muslim families a couple of suburbs down are being persecuted just because of their faith? Can you imagine someone thundering down my door and raiding my place just because I am a white Australian? I hope you can see the insanity of it. Both occupants of both suburbs are Australian citizens. If you're born here citizenship is automatic; if you come from another country and are granted citizenship, you are 'legally' (although this is hypocritical in itself) given the rights of every other Australian regardless of race, religion, or creed. Does everyone forget that Muslims were also killed in 9/11? And God knows how many other places? There have been *many* more Muslims killed than what I label 'us whites'.[34] They are *still* being killed this very second, by the hands of all those that support the Coalition. But

---

[33] HH The Dalai Lama, *The little book of Buddhism,* Rider/Random House, London, 2000, p. 115.

[34] I use these terms with cynicism. Yes, I am what could be labelled 'a white Australian' even though I don't believe in such labels at all. I believe what distinguishes us most is not what we look like, but who we are.

21

how can the human losses of 9/11 ever justify the killing of hundreds of thousands of innocent Afghani and Iraqi civilians??

How many Muslim families who lost loved ones in 9/11 are interviewed on TV? I've never seen one. The commercial media *wants* you to believe that white people are more important, even though the countries of the Coalition are made up of many non-white citizens.

And I wonder; how long had America planned on this invasion? Rumsfeld himself said after 9/11: "Let's bomb Iraq"[35] (they had to do Afghanistan first for political reasons, i.e. it 'looked' better). And how much planning goes into this very Orwellian mass manipulation of the facts? Even though the invasion strategies for Iraq were labelled "incompetent" and the evidence given to justify the invasion were labelled "fraudulent"[36] and even though there were articles published before the war that expressed these points at length, America just pushed on anyway. 'You have the right to freedom of speech', they say to their opponents, and, 'We have the right to do whatever the hell we want'. The Bush government believes that weapons and might equal a 'good war plan'. And it takes decades to build up a war machine such as America has. They have more nuclear, chemical and biological weapons than

---

[35] M Moore, *Fahrenheit 9/11,* documentary, Hopscotch entertainment Pty, Ltd, Westside productions LLC, USA, 2004. Richard Clark relates a conversation he had with Rumsfeld.

[36] R Greenwald, *Uncovered: the whole truth about the Iraq War,* documentary, Caroline Productions Inc., USA, 2004. The extent of this fraudulence is analysed well throughout.

any other country on the planet, and have then declared themselves the WMD[37] police. *But America is the only country that has used nuclear weapons in an act of war, against Japan!*

The U.S. nuked both Nagasaki and Hiroshima, not only killing over 150 thousand innocent civilians, but killing many more over time through the residual effects of radiation poisoning.

It is important to note that the U.S. only 'liberated' the victims of World War II after the other fighting nations were spent; they sat back for years while the horrifying occurred, then swept in when all were weakened and by so doing were able to claim a great deal of power for themselves. America has continued unceasingly since World War II to develop their weaponry. Enver Masud, author of *The War on Islam,* states in a related article, that:

> Meanwhile, the U.S. continues to develop new nuclear weapons, microbes to wipe out entire cities, genetically engineered fungus, and genetically engineered materials—eating bacteria, and to test warheads containing live microbes.[38]

Yet do we ever hear about this? As Chomsky states: "Saddam Hussein was rightly condemned for his failure to comply fully with numerous Security Council resolutions, though less was said about the fact that the US rejected the same resolutions."[39]

---

[37] Weapons of Mass Destruction.

[38] E Masud, 'War on terror or a war on Islam?' *New Dawn Magazine,* No. 88, January-February, 2005, pp. 17-22.

[39] Chomsky, p. 30.

There are reasons why we do not hear about such things unless we actively seek out the information, and it is of crucial importance that we do so. We must consider the true implications of one country dominating all others. On September 17 in 2002 the U.S. announced their imperial grand strategy, which alarmed many. In response—and after more details came to light in mid-October about how close the world came to nuclear war during the Cuban missile crisis—the UN Disarmament Committee acted as follows:

> Ten days later, on October 23, the UN Disarmament Committee adopted two crucial resolutions. The first called for stronger measures to prevent the militarization of space and thereby to "avert a grave danger for international peace and security." The second reaffirmed the 1925 Geneva Protocol "prohibiting the use of poisonous gases and bacteriological methods of warfare." Both passed unanimously, with two abstentions: the US and Israel. US abstention amounts to a veto: typically, a double veto, banning the events from reporting and history.[40]

In the case of the second resolution it is not just that the U.S. won't comply; they can in fact implement the use of such weapons, causing untold devastation. In *Weapons of Mass Deception*—a documentary about the manipulation of the American media (and consequently our commercial media) during the Iraq War—Peter Arnett states: "Information dominance requires censorship. Little attention was paid to the U.S. weapons that caused mass destruction, like the legally

---

[40] Chomsky, p. 121.

prohibited cluster bombs that target civilians."[41] You can see stockpiles of some of these Weapons of Mass Destruction on Michael Moore's film: *Bowling for Columbine.*

It takes a lot of manipulation to 'sell' an illegal war. Arnett continues: "When you look at the war in Iraq it's at times impossible to separate media, CIA, PR firms, government ... it all came together."[42]

The Bush II government's intention is to divide the world. Divide and conquer. Not just by supporting Pakistan, who backed the Taliban, while at the same time fighting *against* the Taliban; or by supporting Saddam, until it was no longer in their interests. Nor through their extensive training of terrorists, and their history of state sponsored terrorism. Just look at the apparently 'democratically elected' government of Iraq—even some war criminals were given power! Iraq is losing 8 billion dollars of oil revenue a year through mismanagement and dodgy dealings. Many people in Iraq have no oil, no electricity, no water, no shelter, no rights, no security, and again, this is no less true in Afghanistan.

But it is not only the Middle East that the U.S. seeks to divide. They suppress the rise of many possible socialist governments throughout the world, keeping millions collectively beyond the reach of democracy, and they've been doing it for decades. This latest 'war on terror' is

---

[41] D Schechter, *Weapons of Mass Deception,* documentary, WMD GlobalVision LP, USA, 2004. Peter Arnett discusses the media coverage of the Iraq War.

[42] Schechter, 2004.

merely the reaffirmed continuum of a terrorist campaign led *by* the U.S. as part of their ongoing quest for global domination.

> The leaders of the current Bush administration—mostly recycled from more reactionary sectors of the Reagan-Bush I administrations—provided sufficiently clear illustrations during their earlier stints in office. When the traditional regime of violence and repression was challenged by the Church and other miscreants in the Central American domains of US power, the Reagan administration responded with a "war on terror," declared as soon as it took office in 1981. Not surprisingly, the US initiative instantly became a terrorist war—a campaign of slaughter, torture, and barbarism—that soon extended to other regions of the world as well.[43]

These acts of terror also applied to 'other regions of the world' as just referred to, includes support for brutal past dictators such as Suharto (Indonesia) and the Khmer Rouge (Cambodia). This is only the names of *two* madmen that the U.S. has backed for its own purposes; there are many more. An example of how this terror is implemented is as follows (continuing from the previous quote):

> In one country, Nicaragua, Washington had lost control of the armed forces that had traditionally subdued the region's population, one of the bitter legacies of Wilsonian idealism. The US-backed Somoza dictatorship was overthrown by the Sandinista rebels, and the murderous National Guard was dismantled. Therefore Nicaragua had to be subjected to a campaign of international terrorism

---

[43] Chomsky, pp. 8-9.

that left the country in ruins.[44]

When Nicaragua took their case to the UN Security Council—after the U.S. rejected orders to cease operations given by the World Court—the U.S. vetoed the decision. When Nicaragua went to the UN General Assembly, the U.S. had opposed the resolution (to obey international law). "Little of this was even reported, and the matter has disappeared from history."[45] If Nicaraguans were to vote in a government that the U.S. did not approve of (as in one that the U.S. couldn't control) " … then Nicaragua will again be considered a state that supports terrorism, with the penalties that ensue, which are not trivial."[46] You can see that this strategy is still regularly applied by the U.S. government.

You may well ask why the U.S. would go to such extreme lengths to keep poor countries such as Nicaragua under such tight control. There are many reasons: to have control over their air space; to build air bases; to control the country's assets and resources; to implement regional strategies to gain control of surrounding countries; or to simply crush any progression towards democracy so that those countries do not "infect" other nations, as was the case here.[47] Obviously a free living nation would not want a foreign country in control of their resources and land, therefore repression of freedom is the only way that the U.S. can guarantee that control. Also, because this strategy

---

[44] Chomsky, p. 9.
[45] Chomsky, p. 102.
[46] Chomsky, p. 105.
[47] Chomsky, p. 99.

reaches across the globe, (indeed implemented in some form in every country where it is possible), it means that the U.S. has soldiers in over 150 countries, and air bases in all strategic circles; certainly this is necessary for a country that wants sole domination of the world.

To maintain this domination it is also important for the U.S. to control its own people. Public opinion is often steered by the media; fear tactics are regularly applied intending to create moral divisions within societies.

> The Republicans have a coherent electoral strategy. They seek to create a popular base for social reaction and militarism by sponsoring Christian fundamentalism and utilizing so-called 'wedge' issues such as gay marriage, abortion and school prayer.[48]

Haven't we seen this recently in our own country? Howard has also fuelled these very same debates to divide Australia. Howard is friends with Bush. Bush is a fundamentalist Christian. Many of the Americans who back these wars are fundamentalist Christians; they call themselves 'born-agains'. These Christians believe that they are the 'chosen ones' who will be saved by their perceived 'God' when the supposed final battle takes place (Armageddon). At this time every non-Christian will be destroyed, or burn forever in hell, even all those non-Christian infants—now that doesn't seem very Christ-like to me. But it is on this premise that they are trying to 'save (convert) us'. Yet their plan needs many wars, much upheaval and great destruction to occur

---

[48] The world socialist website, 'The US election will intensify', *Labor Review*, The Victorian Labor College, No. 41, Autumn, 2005, pp. 12-14.

before this prophecy can be fulfilled.

When any individuals' or groups' beliefs are put into force and their beliefs cause pain to others, it is a terrible and disastrous choice. I believe *all* religions need to employ empathy and compassion about these situations: the pain caused for women denied the right to an abortion[49] particularly if pregnancy occurs through rape; the pain suffered by same-sex partners who are continually discriminated against; the unending guilt felt by those who are convinced that they are sinners who will forever burn in hell; the pain of someone judging you without knowing your circumstances or the pain of someone bombing, killing or starving you because you believe differently than they do. I can promise you that none of my beliefs would ever intentionally hurt a single soul. To hold beliefs that cause others pain is just not acceptable. Many injustices are committed in the name of religion.

No matter under what banner or for what reason, it is of utmost importance to monitor human rights abuses regardless of who is doing the abusing and to act in the best interests of the masses at large who are being persecuted.

But this can only be done with the right intentions and never for personal gain. And just as religious beliefs can

---

[49] For those who do not believe in the right to abortion, for reasons such as: 'Every life has a right to live/be born', I ask, 'What about the right of the mother to live a sane and healthy life, having the right to decide for herself?' In many instances of rape, it may be more humane to give the mother the right to an abortion than to force her to carry the baby full term.

never excuse human rights abuses, we also cannot persecute the majority of constituents of any given religion for the fanatical action of the few, such as is occurring with the Islamic faith. Coalition governments have portrayed a distorted view of Muslim culture throughout our mainstream media, without having explored the subject or having any idea about what the Muslim culture actually is.

How do we have the gall to say that we are 'saving' Muslims whilst simultaneously bombing them and completely disrespecting their belief system???

Wake Up World!!

This is Orwell's *1984* in action. Don't let it fool you. What you hear the leaders of the Coalition saying, please know that the opposite is actually true. Now let's get back to some actual truth. Although I am no scholar on the principles of Islam, I do know some essential facts:

1) When Mohammed was spreading the word of Islam (c 610 onwards)—by offering the choice of the Islamic faith, *not through military force*— he not only allowed Christians and Jews to continue practising their faith, he studied alongside them. The later conquerors, Persians and Mongols among them, were far more brutal rulers than Mohammed himself. It is due to the work of the earliest Islamist scholars, including Christian and Jewish scholars of that time, who studied and interpreted the scriptures of the ancient Greeks, among other things, that we have what is known today as civilization. Islam

invoked unity amongst the Arab people, who had previously worshipped multiple gods with much fighting occurring between different tribes. The cities of Islam were the first to have running water, medicine, and social justice laws. Europe was still in the dark ages and the Renaissance did not seed there until 600 years after Baghdad was a great city.[50] The knowledge of Islam is entrenched in our culture; it is present in our language, our social, scientific and mathematical laws, just to mention a few. After horrendous assaults on the Muslim culture—whereby much knowledge was gained and integrated—those same Europeans tried to eradicate and defile the name of Islam, and there is no real acknowledgement in the West that any such influence existed. This makes the West's phobia of Islam even more paradoxical; we have no appreciation of our own roots.

2) The Islamic religion stems directly from the Christian and Judaist faiths. The term 'Allah' is simply the Arab word for God.

3) The divide between Shiites and Sunnis only occurred when two groups disagreed over who should rule Islam after Mohammed's death; a relative of Mohammed, or a non-relative. Obviously the dispute has grown to become much more, but it started here.[51]

Christianity, like Islam, could be used by fundamentalists and turned into something that borders

---

[50] R Gardner, *Islam: Empire of Faith,* documentary, Gardner films Inc./PBS, USA, 2000.
[51] Gardner, 2000.

on fanaticism. The written materials in both the Bible and the Koran have been used to justify human rights abuses. But are the Christian Right in America, (who were instrumental in the re-election of George Bush), any better or different than the fundamentalist Islamists? Both use religion as a reason to hate and persecute those who do not believe the same as they do. Both use their beliefs to justify inhumane behaviour. Both oppress women and freedom of speech; both deny compassion to their enemies. But remember, fundamentalists always tend to come in small bunches. It is obvious that most of the 1 billion people who follow the Muslim faith do not incite violence or harm others. If that were so you would certainly know about it! There are many people that follow the Christian and Muslim faiths and live by their main ideals to not harm *even* their enemies. Many Christians and Muslims use their religion as a framework for being decent human beings. The problem is that we shouldn't need religion to stop people killing each other; in fact, it is in the name of religion that killing often takes place. But it is the conservative Australians that voted to kill, not the Muslims. No Muslim voted to kill *us*. Please remember that.

I have never seen a Muslim in Australia who didn't seem peaceful. But do you know there are many Muslims here who are called 'terrorists' from passing motorists? To the women wearing the hijab? That the racism inherent in Australian history is rearing its ugly head on a daily basis?[52]

---

[52] ABC, *Compass: Islam on parade*, television program, Australia, 16 October 2005. Young Australian Muslims describe the racism they've experienced.

> I don't need a passport to walk on this earth,
> anywhere I go cause I was made of this earth, I'm
> born of this earth, I breathe of this earth, and even
> with the pain I believe in this earth …
> Cause every bit of land is a holy land and every drop
> a water is a holy water and every single child is a son
> or a daughter of the one earth mama and the one
> earth papa, so don't tell a man that he can't come
> here cause he got brown eyes and a wavy kinda hair
> and don't tell a woman that she can't go there
> because she prays a little different to a God up there
> …[53]

We have become so prejudiced against a race of people which means we clearly have not learnt from the past. I mean, imagine if we started to attack another culture here, say the Chinese, Greeks or Italians? Saying their culture is 'un-Australian'? Saying they don't have Australian 'values'? Can you imagine? The whole point of having a multicultural society is that you embrace *all* cultures. We, as a country, have used the labour of those foreigners who boosted our economy and enriched the nation. But we also start to see and accept other value systems, and we use our multiculturalism to invite in even more money, from tourism. In Melbourne alone, there are over 150 different religious/cultural groups. To pick out one of these religions/cultures and start all this crap of 'we'll throw you out of the country if you don't have Australian values' is absolute nonsense. I mean what values are they talking about anyway: persecution, torture, oppression, lying? For really these are the values that the Australian government currently represents.

---

[53] Michael Franti & Spearhead, *Hello Bonjour,* 2006.

There is much hypocrisy evident in the beliefs of some in our society. I've heard some people say as a justification for the wars in the Middle East, that: 'But the Muslims treat their women so terribly, so at least we're liberating them'.[54] This abuse of women is true in some cases and obviously it is intolerable. But how are women treated in this country? It is not up to us to change Islamic law; it is up to those whom the laws affect. Many women and men are fighting hard to bring more equality into the laws of those countries, and of course we need to support them in this. The family law in some Middle Eastern countries (created by men, and only *their* interpretation of the Koran), is barbaric by Western (or anyone's) standards: women cannot legally divorce, can be forced into sex and duty, can be battered 'legally'. There are terrible punishments for women, who can be lashed, stoned or imprisoned after being raped (for breaking an Islamic law of being alone with a man not their husband!)—this law is often enforced in Saudi Arabia, an ally of the U.S.!! These laws are obviously a gross violation of women's human rights.

Yes, it's true that our system is nowhere near as brutal but that doesn't mean there aren't ignored and battered women in Australia too (not to mention in many other 'wealthy' and 'democratic' countries). We have one of the highest suicide and domestic violence rates in the world, not to mention sexual assault. We have child abuse that is prevalent, and not just in Black Australia! (As the mainstream media would have us think.) And we have a society that barely talks about it. Of 100% of

---

[54] The fact is nothing the Coalition has done has improved the rights of women in the Middle East; if anything, the lack of security has made many women much more vulnerable.

reported rapes in Melbourne (and remember many aren't reported), up to 90% of cases never make it to court because the legal processes are too traumatic for the victims. This is a disastrous situation by anyone's standards, and certainly not reflective of a fair and democratic society.

We can protest against those laws in countries overseas, but we cannot preach that which we ourselves, do not even uphold.

****

> Armagedon is a deadly day, Armagedon is a deadly way, they comin for you everyday while senators on a holiday, the Army recruiters in the parking lot, hustling the kids there jugglin pot, listen young man listen to my plan gonna make you money gonna make you a man, Bom Bom, here's what you get, an M-16 and a Kevlar vest, you might come home with one less leg, but this thing will surely keep a bullet out your chest so come on, come on, sign up come on, this ones nothing like Vietnam, except for the bullets, except for the bombs, except for the youth that's gone, so we keep it on til ya coming home ... [55]

The dictators of the West clothe themselves in self-piety; they do everything in the name of: 'for the country' or 'for our fellow man'. They even had the gall to call the invasion of Iraq: 'Operation Iraqi Freedom'. And how free is Iraq now, many years later? They called the mission—the first barrage of bombings— 'Shock and Awe' for God's sake! Isn't it obvious

---

[55] Michael Franti & Spearhead, *Light Up Ya Lighter,* 2006.

people? The 'Coalition of the Willing' is the 'Coalition of the Killing', at home, and abroad. And what about Abu Grahib? Have you *seen* the pictures? *Do you understand that our country supports the deliberate torture of our fellow human beings?*

> These other questioners saw to it that he was in constant slight pain, but it was not chiefly pain that they relied on. They slapped his face, wrung his ears, pulled his hair ... shone glaring lights in his face until his eyes ran with water; but the aim of this was simply to humiliate him and destroy his power of arguing and reasoning. Their real weapon was the merciless questioning that went on and on, hour after hour, tripping him up, laying traps for him, twisting everything that he said, convicting him at every step of lies and self-contradiction, until he began weeping as much from shame as from nervous fatigue.[56]

How close is this fictional description of torture in Orwell's *1984* to an accurate description of what occurs in Guantanamo Bay and other such prisons? In the 'Ministry of Love' in *1984* lights are kept on for 24 hours a day.[57] Prisoners who have been tortured by the Coalition report this method also. There are many brutal methods currently being used on people in the 'rendition'[58] program; acts so terrible you could not fathom.

---

[56] Orwell, *1984,* pp. 253-254.

[57] Orwell, p. 241.

[58] This term is used to describe the secret movement by the U.S. of prisoners throughout the world. They are moved to countries where rules against the use of torture are weak or non-existent.

To even be in the ballpark of the bleak totalitarian world of *1984* is mind-boggling. Yet we are allowing these rulers to create such a world. A mean twisted world where everyone is set against each other. As long as these rulers have us hating the Muslims and them hating us, they can continue to do whatever they damn well like. It's that divide and conquer thing. They'll continue killing while we argue about whether or not head scarves should be worn in a democratic, multicultural country. *Please Wake Up World!!*

The Coalition are creating nothing but pain; destroying the birthplace of civilization in the *name* of civilization.

Holy Universe, *I* feel violated, for them and for me. You see, not in my name. Dear God, John Howard, not in my name. How dare you participate in the grilling and the torture and the broken houses and the broken towns and the broken faces of those who pick up their dead from the ground? How dare you support a war against international law? How dare you detain people who have fled from their broken countries and put them like animals in a cage and watch them rot and go insane? How dare you in my name and in the name of this country? You are as un-Australian as it gets. You are a white conservative, in a long line of white conservatives. You don't get at all that the core of this country is black, is Aboriginal. There are lifetimes of love and care and heart preserved into the soil of this country. There is a beautiful race of people here with so much wisdom in their ancestry and culture. Even if you, the reader, are judging how the Indigenous people lived before we invaded, and even now, you cannot deny that this has always been a black country. Whites are like a disease; a plague that came in and settled on the land.

We brought with us our curses, our alcohol, our illnesses. We brought our horrible shame, of every invasion we have instigated in England's name. Carving our caricature of violence and greed, killing the spirit and watching it bleed, but some things I believe will never die; open the passion in our hearts and we don't even need to try.

Aside from all these current abominations, I have cried many tears for the terrible persecution that we *still* ignore, upon the original peoples of this land. We are only a scratch on the surface. It's been just over 200 years, compared with tens of thousands of years that *they* lived here. We've come in, done unspeakable things and even today, we still do unspeakable things.

Can we honestly say that the Indigenous people have been better off since England's invasion? (The actual goal was annihilation.) How many Indigenous people do we see on what we now call 'our' streets? We can't just say: 'Oh we want to reconcile' unless we're actually willing to *do* something to help make this happen. But let's face it, many 'Australians' out there see no and hear no. But do they know how the government is treating these people? Can you imagine being asked to put your garbage out so that you can get a petrol bowser for your town? How humiliating that is? Can you imagine that happening to white folk, for instance? And we go on and on about 'how disgraceful the abuse is in some Indigenous communities'. Yes, it is terrible. But we are the ones who helped to create this! We are still contributing to it through our own lack of responsibility. And as for the customs that were in place before we invaded? I do not know, but that's the point; what I do not know I certainly do not have the right to judge.

Again, I believe it should be mandatory for all cultures and religions to uphold human rights and human decency. Indigenous perpetrators cannot be allowed to hide behind traditional law if that law strips another of their rights. I do not know to what extent this occurred before England invaded.

But this is what we know now:

We *know* we have displaced a people, causing the destruction of their culture, languages and wisdom, giving them no access to their natural resources (on which the Indigenous had obviously survived for millennia), breaking up their families, stealing their land, their children (can you imagine?), enslaving and indoctrinating them, then many years later offering some pathetic amount of welfare, done through the white man's papers, and not integrating any awareness of the cultural differences, and without offering enough funds or creating access to support systems and resources such as counselling, rehabilitation, education actually suitable to its recipients and inclusive of Indigenous culture, crisis support, cultural support, opportunities for youth, food and shelter, and sexual health centres. (Much of the welfare systems for non-Indigenous Australians are grossly under funded too, but at least they are there.) We have ensured that those people, especially in the remoter communities, have no chance of rising out of poverty, so long as they are fed on broken promises. And what about the alcohol? When you feel persecuted and have every right to feel that way, when there is discrimination everywhere you turn, when those around you have endured the same mistreatment—creating self-hatred and self-abuse in some, and/or abuse towards others—and then you add alcohol on top of all that vulnerability to addiction, what is likely to happen? It is no wonder some Indigenous are so brutal to their own. To some of them, it is all they've known. But you must understand it was the white people that originally *brought* the alcohol, along with many other poisons, much disease, and much brutality.

We talk about housing to a people that have lived under the stars for millennia. We offer welfare where their natural land was plentiful for all. The ancestry of the people of this country is what whites have trodden upon and we cannot separate their situation now from the reality of their history, from the reality of our own denial to do anything about this epidemic problem. We must all voice our disgust at a national level. We treat our pets better than we treat our Indigenous, whilst parading our invasion flag and saying how much we 'love' our country. Howard encourages whom I'll refer to as 'tarts and thugs'[59] to dress up and wear the Australian flag in 'colourful ways' (his words). Our flag is merely a representation of England's invasion, still showing no recognition of Black Australia. But how do *we* treat the land? Here's an example of how much we 'love' our country: uranium mining uses up to 42 million litres of water *a day*.[60] Yet we have a water crisis.

---

[59] I am stereotypically referring to those who get attention at major events (usually sporting) by girls wearing the flag as a boob-tube or mini-skirt and men using it—usually in groups—as a way to invoke a sense of patriotism and/or racism.

[60] ABC, *We of little voice*, television program, Australia, 18 June 2007.

A prolific amount of radioactive waste has been spilt through uranium mining, poisoning water systems on this sacred land, land the Indigenous have never exploited. Now Howard wants us to embrace nuclear power, as if uranium mining isn't doing enough damage. And Australia is one of the largest exporters of uranium in the world.

We are a segregated nation, in every aspect of the word. There is even an Indigenous footy show on Channel 31—*The Marngrook Footy Show*—which is great, but surely this should be aired to the same amount of viewers as *The Footy Show* on Channel 9 or at the very least be given a link from the show. We glorify Indigenous players on the field whilst still failing to recognise the needs of their race in their own country. Sure, Indigenous people can get an education, follow up resources, strive to become their very best and rise above oppression. There are many doing great work all over Australia, through education and cultural gatherings, etc., but they are doing so with little or no support from either governments or the wider Australian public.

Yes, Indigenous people need to be empowered, but just like every other human on the planet; they will find it difficult to do so within an inherently discriminatory system.

If you want to see this segregation in action, talk to the tourists visiting the Northern Territory who have no idea about the state of our Indigenous affairs until they are asked to sign a document when they buy alcohol that states they won't sell those drinks to Aborigines. Or look for the token alcoholics in your capital city. Please do not blame any Indigenous people for their addiction to alcohol and other substances. How well would you fare in their situation? With a government that just doesn't care?? Our Indigenous are the forgotten people and few in the world ever hear of their story (although there are numerous reports made by United Nations bodies that raise concern about the human rights issues here; an international organisation that takes more interest in this problem than Australia itself); still many tourists happily purchase Indigenous art. We destroy their culture as best we can, and then start selling it.

Of course, it is up to each individual to be responsible for themselves; I am simply pointing out that the greater the difficulties that one endures, the harder this may be for one to do. Understanding the context in which people suffer is crucial if help is to be offered and received.

The reality is that the stealing of children from their families only ceased *40 odd years ago!!* When England invaded Australia they wiped out at least 90% of the Indigenous race on the mainland and close to (if not actually) all Aboriginals in Tasmania, then forced the remaining folk into slavery, and later on, assimilation. Can you imagine a race of people doing this to you? If you can, you know how horrific what we did as a country is. There is barely a new generation of Indigenous children who weren't taken from their families, for the purposes of 'breeding' them with whites so as to integrate them with white society. Assimilation is in fact an elongated form of genocide.

The amount of mistreatment inflicted upon the Aboriginal people of this land by the powers that be, has a long and painful history. Many cases of discrimination (some of which has caused fatalities) still occur today. And just as with the refugees, *we* have no right to judge the behaviour of these people when we have no idea of the weight of suffering inherent in our Indigenous population.

It utterly horrifies me; the incredible history of white men taking over the world. They have discovered and then destroyed so much culture. But it's only in dictatorships that absolute power is held over the people. Therefore it is those people living in relative peace and comfort that support the destructiveness that can become the most dangerous. These people want to preserve *their* way of life, even at the expense of the rest of the world. But where we have the right to vote, we have the responsibility to vote and it's imperative we vote for leaders who *will act humanely*. Why isn't it already mandatory that our own government upholds human rights? Oh, that's right, it is; there *are* international laws that apply to us, and we are breaking them! Yet regardless of this, people voted Howard back in. And I wonder; would they like to be bombed because someone overseas had had enough of Howard's 'dictatorship'? If it's about security, and they are scared, why would they create their own nightmare? Because harming people—attacking them with no just cause—is certainly not a good option if you want to stay safe. Here's what Howard voters are really supporting.

Human Rights Violations.

Australia's got it on a few counts:

1) We have Indigenous people in our country

living in third world conditions.

2) We have detained innocent people against their will and held them indefinitely in appalling conditions.

3) We are persecuting our fellow Australians in the Muslim community, simply because of their choice of religion.

4) We have supported a war without the approval of the United Nations (UN). An illegal war where we (the Coalition) torture people and dismantle a country based on hearsay, not facts.

A person who loves their country knows the importance of defying its unhealthy governance. Nothing is more truly patriotic.[61] Unfortunately Australia's patriotism is steeped in a sense of self-serving righteousness; a basic ingredient for fascism. But there is one ultimate fact I know:

If you don't want it done to you, don't ever let it be done to anyone else.

And I don't have to follow a religion to understand that, I just have to be human.

> I may not believe in God
> Does it mean I'm a lesser person?
> I still have a heart
> And I know what it feels like to be broken
> …
> I'm not concerned with religion
> After all it's what's inside that matters most[62]

---

[61] Greenwald, 2004. Joseph Wilson discusses the importance of having accountability in government.

[62] The Living End, *Raise the alarm,* music album, White

44

It doesn't take a belief in God for one to want peace for all humanity (though many may aspire to this by believing in God). To want peace for all beings comes from respecting and appreciating all life.

The reason I am so passionate about humanity is because I am so incredibly thankful for all the freedoms that I have, even the freedom to write this. I just want to do all that I can in this lifetime, to increase and All Atoms help me make aware, for goodness sake, what are we doing? *We cannot treat people this way!* All over the world, this must end. The fact that so many are suffering through this needless persecution makes … me … feel … ill. The one thing that keeps me from being overwhelmed is my will to do all that I can to stop it. And it works. I feel incredibly content with my decision to support human rights. *As a human being, it seems the only sane choice.*

Of course I would much rather live in a peaceful world than have to speak the truth of an unjust one. Since the beginning of our time humans have struggled with power and with peace. It is only when we accept that we are all 'stakeholders' in this world, when we all accept the responsibility of upholding human rights, being human ourselves, that we will stop allowing the few to destroy the many. Your input alone is the first step.

"Tolerance or violence? And the whole world goes to war
Is one enough or is one too many before we say no more?"[63]

Noise, Chris Cheney, Dew Process, 2008.
[63] Michael Franti & Spearhead, *Tolerance,* 2006.

Ideas and Solutions:

- Seek information on the history of Islam. Look at the parallels between the cities Islam created, and our own democracy.
- All we have to do to turn the tides in favour of human rights is to communicate it emphatically to all people, including those in power. You can email and write letters to any member of the government, demanding that justice be sought for any issue you feel is valuable. How easy is it to write an email?
- If you are passionate enough about social justice issues, become an independent, or join the Greens.
- Apologise on behalf of our country to our Indigenous and our Muslim residents whenever you get the opportunity.
- It is important to remember that America and Australia are two of the youngest countries in the world. Both slaughtered the Indigenous populations to claim the land. Both have an extensive history of conquering and of war (descending from England) and both have created (at least for the majority of their citizens) an empty wasteful culture, unlike the nations we are attacking now which have thousands of years of history, and rich complex cultures. We must expand our knowledge on these matters.
- There are many people who have fled from war in Australia right here, right now. A $5-10 a month donation, or some of that tinned food in your cupboard, could be feeding many families in urgent need. You can donate to the Asylum

Seeker Resource Centre.

- I strongly encourage you to join, or at least check out, the Get-Up campaign. This is a non-partisan grass-roots movement in Australia taking positive and practical action on many important issues.
- Bring awareness to other Australians about the struggles of our Indigenous people whenever possible. The Northern Territory intervention is only creating more fear; why use the military when your goal is to protect children? It is horrendous. These communities need support and funding, not soldiers. Many of these communities have been neglected for decades and beyond; what is needed is reconciliation and a strong Indigenous voice in the Australian government.

Chapter 3 – Understanding

It is amazing how the media dictates our lives in such a way that one week we are asked to be concerned about this and the next week we are asked to be concerned about something else. In the end we may just want to tune out altogether. But I believe the time has come for us to realise the truth; at a deep level we *are* concerned about *all* of it. I believe it is time for us to tune in.

The reason I cannot sit here on my democratic throne, living on top of the world, oblivious to the outside is simply because I *know* this is only the blessing of fate and circumstance. If I came to be born in Africa, what perils may I suffer there? If I was to be born in China, what perils would I suffer there? If I was born a koala, or a whale, or a lamb, what perils do I suffer there? You see, it is *human beings* who are responsible for the devastation of natural resources, the devastation of human lives, the devastation of thousands of species, and possibly the future devastation of the planet itself. I am not talking about environmental disaster here; I am talking of human disaster.

I cannot live without caring about life itself.
I cannot look at human suffering and say 'that's ok, there's nothing I can do about it anyway'.

So I farther implore you to look deeply within, to get the message—if you haven't already—that what happens to others *does* require our care and our understanding not just for others' sake, but for our own as well. Judgment not only increases our pain but also our feelings of separation. We cannot accept for others what we wouldn't accept for ourselves, without being inhumane, or separated from our own hearts and souls.

Right now, I want to explore the issue of suicide bombers. And I ask you to consider this: If your country was invaded or occupied, therefore suffering a terrible fate, how far would you go to retaliate; to protect your family? If you truly believed that your country, your honour, your people, your religion, were more important than your own life, could you sacrifice it? Would you sacrifice it if you felt you had any other choice? Of course you wouldn't! Please understand that suicide bombings would not occur if those people, human beings just like you, felt they had *any other choice.*

It is absolutely horrendous that humans are put into such a position where they feel they have no other choice but to kill themselves and others. But it disgusts me that Bush and Howard have participated in the killings of many more hundreds of thousands of people, yet here they are, still in power, and nobody saying a word. They are not labelled in the mainstream media as either terrorists or war criminals, yet they both, irrefutably, are.

How we allow these guys to stay in power I do not understand. Try *not* invading a country or oppressing people, try allowing people to live their lives in peace, see how many suicide bombers you would get then.

Yes, it is terrible that people do such things. But how do they come to it? Many Taliban members are trained in refugee camps from a very young age, raised without women, and given no formal education. Many children in war torn countries are forced to deal with constant uncertainty, violence and hatred, they may inevitably fall into fighting, and often this may be the only way that they can actually survive.

Remember, it is the Bush administration itself that *has* condoned, and *is* condoning, the most brutal torture of Muslims in the name of the 'war on terror'. The barbarity of these crimes only adds to the gulf of pain already being inflicted. The majority of suspects interrogated are given over to the Coalition by Afghani or Iraqi warlords (who are paid in cash grants) and not captured by Coalition soldiers. Many who are tortured are innocent, so why torture them? Well, for one, because Bush and co. need to show the world what will happen to all those who come into conflict with the American agenda. They also want to obtain 'information' by any means necessary, yet obviously if one is being tortured one would say anything one thought could end it, making many of these so-called 'confessions' extremely dubious.[64] This is how far the U.S. will go to secure their power in the world. Commit terror beyond your wildest fears.[65] This is the reality. Knowing this, how now do you view Muslims and 'terrorists'? Can you not see what might drive people to blow themselves and others up? Tell me you can see the difference between the oppressors and the oppressed?

---

[64] David Rose, author of *Guantanamo: America's war on human rights* claims that many prisoners that were tortured were also asked to act as spy agents for the U.S.

[65] Methods of torture used against Muslims include acts which attempt to denigrate Islam, such as: forced sex acts, displaying of pornography, and urination on the Koran, in conjunction with the regular barbaric methods including prolonged beatings, deprivation (of food, water, sleep etc.), water boarding (simulated drowning), electric shock and relentless interrogation.

The situation between Israel and Palestine is a perfect example of how people come to be suicide bombers. I did not understand this conflict many years ago. I couldn't figure out from all the news reports who was oppressing who, so I asked a lot of questions and read a lot of reports and it didn't take too long to figure it out. It is quite simple. The U.S. declared the state of Israel after World War II, as a homeland for the Jews, but this 'state' was claimed on Palestinian land, completely displacing the many Palestinians who lived there! Yes, the Jewish people (along with many others who are rarely mentioned) suffered terribly under Hitler; yes, they deserve the right to live in peace and a place to live; and yes, the Israelis say that Palestine is their rightful homeland, but how does this justify the ongoing oppression of the Palestinian people?

There are currently *over 5 million* Palestinians displaced throughout the world, with many countries punished (via sanctions, trade embargos etc.) by the U.S. government (and allies) if Palestinian refugees are offered asylum. They are discriminated against everywhere they go yet they are not allowed to return to the only home they know.

Israel is backed by America. They have been armed by America (supplied with U.S. weapons and military technology, among other things) as part of their master plan for the Middle East. The Palestinians have very few weapons, no army, and are utterly defenceless against the Israeli forces comprising of hundreds of thousands of soldiers, vast weaponry and the latest military technology. They are heavily sanctioned and like many in occupied countries are always in a perpetual struggle against starvation. Basic supplies that rich societies take for granted can become life and death issues for those who are oppressed. In protest and retaliation and without access to other conventional avenues of defence or attack some Palestinians have acted as suicide bombers in Israel. Then Israel built a huge wall and many tunnel systems with security check points to and from Palestine so that the Israelis can get into Palestine but the Palestinians can't get out! Meanwhile Israel continues its oppressive tactics, regular air bombings among them, and gains even more control. It is truly disgusting the continuous brutality the American and Israeli governments have inflicted upon the people of Palestine. In the writing of this book the Palestinian situation has only worsened. The Fatah group—which took power from the legitimately elected Hamas—is American backed. So when you hear about the Israeli/Palestinian peace talks, you are looking at two American backed groups, with Hamas now deemed a terrorist organisation even though they have been fighting for Palestinian freedom for decades now.

Please note in this dialogue that I'm also very sorry to any Israeli people who have suffered loss at a Palestinians hand; pain is pain in any language. Almost all conflicts cause innocent civilians to be hurt or killed on both sides. I just wish in this case that their countries need for self-protection didn't involve implementing actions which cause ongoing suffering for *most* Palestinians.

As I have said, people do not blow themselves up because they live in happy democratic places where they are treated fairly. People do not do anything for no reason. I am not saying all this to justify the actions of suicide bombers, because human rights need to be upheld *by all people,* but many of us have little idea of what is really going on, and to judge what we do not understand, is not only arrogant, but futile. If you look deep into your heart and imagine the perils of living with war, and truly allow yourself to even glimpse upon the horrific nature of war, then you may begin to lose your judgments of people who act and react to circumstances you cannot comprehend.

There are obviously many, many, many more people living with war who don't hurt others, and are just doing all they can to survive; praying for an end to the suffering. Our heartstrings must vibrate for all those suffering. We must feel and acknowledge the terrible state of things.

The rich and the free who are doing the oppressing, yes, we have a grave responsibility to judge their acts, because they are breaking the law that governs all of us: the law of Humanity.

This law is defied by all those who profit from war.

Chapter 4 – What can you do?

*"... there is no cure and no improving of the world that does
not begin with the individual himself ... "*[66]

What can you do? In a conflicted world ...

Ok. So, you are one human being in a planet of over 6
billion. You may not think that you could clear up all
the bad stuff in this world, but yet, why not? Praying for
World Peace and thinking about it every day I believe
can have a powerful effect on the global consciousness,
not to mention on you! But even without doing this, we
can certainly communicate thoughts of light and love to
all those around us. Regardless of external forces, we
can work on the betterment of our own humanity. If we
all learnt to do this, you begin to see how achievable
global healing could be. The most crucial thing to know
is that everything you do affects the world around you.
Every bug you tread on, every blade of grass you
squash; it all has an effect on your external
environment. Think about every smile you give or every
smile you receive, or every time you're pissed off and
probably quashed many a stranger. Everything you do
has an effect.

*One person can make a difference and one person
always does.*

If you care about humanity you can make a huge
difference just by talking about it; every discussion
raises awareness and you don't know how far that could

---

[66] CG Yung, Two essays on Analytical psychology, as quoted
by Ivarna Kalinkova, *The Wisdom Well,* Quarto, 2003, p. 62.

reach. Be willing to look into world affairs and try to distinguish propaganda from underlying truths. We have way too many people in the capitalist countries ignoring the reality of suffering in our world. But to deny the reality of human/earth suffering is the most disastrous choice of all. Why? Because to deny the existence of a fellow human's rights pretty much denies you of your heart. And to deny the hurt of our planet pretty much vanquishes it too.

I have attempted to make clear some of these issues in the preceding chapters. There is much apathy in Australia though things are starting to move and I pray will continue to move in a more humane direction. To understand how to be humane one has only to ask oneself what they would expect others to do if their own rights were being violated.

We must make others aware of their own humanity. If we want to be cared for, we have to care for others.

The importance of humanity has been discussed throughout the ages. Socrates states, as written in Plato's *The Republic:*

> So it wasn't a wise man who said that justice is to give every man his due, if what he meant by it was that the just man should harm his enemies and help his friends. This simply is not true: for as we have seen, it is never right to harm anyone at any time.[67]

Imagine if all people could understand this. Imagine if all people were loved and able to love. Imagine how

_____

[67] Plato, *The Republic,* Penguin Books, England, 1955, p. 15.

magnificent a world could be, if every single living soul was committed to healing themselves and the world. Imagine if creating World Peace was the goal of All People. Imagine if overcoming our own struggles, our own conditioning, is all that is needed to demonstrate and *prove* that every other human being can do this if given the chance. There are many stories of our fellow humans who have overcome great difficulties when the odds were against them. It's time for us to overcome our own.

Yet it is obvious that our government wants you to fall for the capitalist way of life. Mainly they want you to work very hard and to buy and consume a lot so that the rich can just keep on getting richer. Remember, the masses collectively make millionaires, billionaires—just think how much profit is made when one product sold to millions of people has a price rise of 5¢ (which happens a lot more than inflation dictates). It is the wealthy humans in power that decide what's on our TV and in our newspapers (you may know them as Murdoch and Packer). We all need to be taught the skills of reading between the lines.

We need people, just like you, to believe in humanity with all your heart and soul, and recognise that just by being a loving person you are helping the world right now.

"We may even find the solution to hunger and disease
We can bomb the world to pieces, but we can't bomb it into peace"[68]

---

[68] Michael Franti & Spearhead, *Bomb the World,* music album, Everyone Deserves Music, Michael Franti, Boo Boo

And I know we have powers within us. We have the power to vote Howard out, and let's do it quickly! Get him the hell out of there, because he is breeding hatred at a rapid rate, and it is not right, or just, or fair, or rational, or sane. These guys spit out lies as truth and truth as lies. They will do anything to hide their disguise, and we must show them that we are, in fact, paying attention. And I don't mean wait until the next election, I mean get him out now! Don't you understand that *we* are the power? The day we began bombing Baghdad, Holy Universe, I wished that no one would go to work that day. I wished that we would all hang our heads in shame, and listen for every bomb, every bullet, that ripped through every son and every daughter and mother and father and animal. Feel the pain of each violation, which in truth was only the marked continuation of bombing that had been happening for decades, and the rule of a dictator, America itself, put in place. If you could hear every child's cry, or feel their loss of limb, tell me then, how could you still like John Howard?

People say: 'Voters vote for lots of different reasons'. To this I say: 'If your vote involves pre-emptive murder, you are an accomplice'.

There are better ways to do things. Why not talking instead of bombs? We all know why! Greed, money, money, power, money, greed. As insane as it is there are human beings on this planet who seem to have no heart and no soul. Because how could they?

Wax, 2003.

The saying 'war is inevitable' is still a belief held by many and one which doesn't make the world a better place and certainly leaves no room for the possibility of peace. As already mentioned, one must remember that in most destabilised countries, whenever democracy begins to flourish, either the countries own leaders, or other countries with vested interests, have strategies in place to thwart it; an important point to note for those cynics who often coin the aforementioned phrase. (As all that is needed to change this is adequately functioning international laws, and a system of global protection for all citizens of the world.) Yes, there is anger and greed in humans, yes, there are violent tendencies, but all these can be overcome with the development of tolerance and compassion. Some serious changes in the foreign policy format of rich and/or Western countries and some *actual* support given to newly forming democracies (as oppose to resource reaping, i.e. the imposed economic liberalism in the name *of* democracy as is the case now) has great capability of building a fairer world, so it's not that its not possible; it is just not being done! And there is so much more good that we are capable of. We can see this in our scientific technologies (ultimately providing the possibility of clean energy), and medical discoveries (curing pain and disease), and in the Eastern healing methods (offering pathways to inner peace and optimum health). We have access to vast amounts of knowledge. But what good is knowledge if it is not used to farther the growth of human beings? What good is love if it is not used to lead the human race to compassion and peace? There are many people living in peace and contributing to peace every day, but we need as many people contributing to peace as we can get.

Over the course of modern history, there have been significant gains in human rights and democratic control of some sectors of life. These have rarely been the gift of enlightened leaders. They have typically been imposed on states and other power centres by popular struggle.[69]

We must keep this momentum going and remember: We do have the power! Vote Greens, vote Freedom but do not vote for war! That is the worst thing we could vote for. Let's at least be peaceful activists and do what we can through political international pressure to advocate for global peace, to feed the starving, cure the sick, and at the very least, begin to stop the annihilation of our own humanity.

"We cannot hate the haters to set the oppressed free; we can only connect our compassion, across each and every sea"[70]

I am not saying that I have all the answers, far from it. But we do have a lot more choices than we think. Just by limiting the damage in our own world, by treating people with respect, by caring about the state of humanity, by honouring our own hearts, and by voting in a government that does not violate human rights, we are changing the world for the better. Every choice we make affects the world around us, *and* us! If we choose to care about humanity (including ourselves) we are contributing to World Peace.

---

[69] Chomsky, p. 236.
[70] Jess Hieser, *Propaganda,* unreleased music single, Jess Hieser, 2004.

I do not send hate to the leaders who are causing this incredible suffering; I send love and prayers to the humans that *are* suffering. I am writing this to tell you that I believe World Peace is possible, but we must understand this as individuals. Individuals who connect with other individuals creating community units advocating for peace and justice, until our community of peace is global (which it actually is). But we cannot help the world with our heads in the sand, hoping it will just blow over. We must demand peace for ourselves and for everyone in this world. We must pray, want and desire it. The power of thought is amazing, and the more peaceful and loving our thoughts and our actions, the more peace and love we create.

It's amazing how much our own humanity can change the world. We have the choice to create this peace or not. If it's what you want, make all the contributions you can in every way you can. A conversation with someone about human rights at the bus stop may reach 1000s of other people down the track. Each positive change that is made has far-reaching effects. Write letters to government; protest against human rights abuses; join Greenpeace and Human Rights associations. Big or small, *every contribution counts.*

We *all* have a role to play in the healing of human kind. We *all* have a responsibility to fight for human rights.

This book is part of my contribution.

Find your niche.

Ideas and Solutions:

- Don't ever underestimate your own personal power to change yourself and the world for the better.
- Here are some individual actions which could create positive change: use durable and absorbent biodegradable cloth bags instead of plastic for waste disposal and encourage those in your circle to do the same; reduce purchasing plastic wherever possible and email companies requesting they use more environmentally friendly packaging; if you own shares in the stock market, make sure that those companies you've invested in adhere to practices that are both humane and not destructive to the environment and encourage those you know with shares to do the same; start a chain letter which lists the details of humanitarian and environmental non-profit organisations that can be donated to (even if only $5 a month) and deliver to the houses on your street and/or your circle of friends encouraging them to forward on the information.
- Consider that ideas you have about bettering yourself and humanity may be very important information for others to consider also. Talk to those people you feel are open-minded; share your ideas with the community by writing to the local paper or newsletter. Remember all the great ideas in history started with a small seed in an individual's or group's mind.
- People have so many varying interests and it's only natural that some of us feel more strongly about certain issues whether its animal rights,

the environment, famine or the treatment of those in our local aged care facility. If we truly honour that which we feel passionate about we can donate, support, volunteer, and vocalise (through meetings or sending emails) our thoughts on these matters, which is a great contribution to the whole. There are so many wonderful organisations covering a huge range of issues that are working hard to right wrongs and heal crises; the more support they have the stronger their weight in terms of influencing changes in government policy where its needed to truly solve the problems. This is why emailing governments is often just as important as making donations to organisations that are ethical in their work.

PART TWO – The ways we deny our own humanity

Chapter 5 – Lack of awareness

So. You have heard my intellectual and emotional standings (for those who have read thus far), or what could also be described as the torment of my soul. And I wonder at this point, where you are, my reader? How did it make you feel? Do you feel angry? Sad? Do you think I'm a complete and utter lunatic? Do you feel anything at all?

I believe many of us have managed to successfully squash and suppress our feelings of humanity and compassion. The human mind is a powerful thing. We can convince ourselves of certain things and then forget that we created that belief. As Louise L Hay states in her book *You can heal your life:* "We may habitually think the same thought over and over so that it does not seem we are choosing the thought. But we did make the original choice."[71] You can tell when those around you (and yourself) are limiting themselves with their thoughts, and ultimately their beliefs, when they (you) say things such as: 'that's just the way I am' or 'that's just the way it is'.[72] We become so rigid in our thinking that we defiantly cling to *not* changing or not understanding, but as human beings we have great capacity for understanding that could lead to change.

We are each brought up in a particular way and each of us develops our own conditioning based upon this

---

[71] LL Hay, *You can heal your life,* Hayhouse Inc., USA, 2004, p. 5. First published 1984.
[72] See Hay, p. 36.

upbringing. If we were growing up when our country was at war, you can imagine how different our experience would be, and therefore how different our conditioning would be. We have the ability to be open-minded and understand all human viewpoints in all situations. To develop compassion we need to understand this basic truth:

> "All other beings are just like us and they want happiness and dislike suffering."[73]

Can't you see that our apathy is killing our earth and our fellow humans? We are in need of *huge* amounts of humanity.

The best way to increase your own humanity is to become self-aware.

Rather than react to the circumstances around you, be aware of why you are in them in the first place. Are you learning *from* life or are you reacting *to* life? Being self-aware means to recognise and understand you; the being that has lived and grown to get to this point right now. What has moulded you? What are the key contributing factors? The most powerful influence probably comes from our parents and families. So many of us grow up, in happy or unhappy homes, with the constant influence of those who gave birth to us, or who raised us. Many young people look up to adults as their role models and strive to fill the shoes of those role models. It is only when they become adults themselves that they realise being an adult does not necessarily mean that one is

---

[73] HH The Dalai Lama, *The little book of Wisdom*, Rider/Random House, London, 2000, p. 127.

wise, or in control, or even happy. Just look at your own parent's patterns (anger, control, discipline—or lack of) and look at your own. *It's up to you who you actually become.*

We can recognise the better qualities of our families and choose to develop those traits; we can learn about our parents and their history and in so doing gain an understanding of the context of our lives. This knowledge can help us to become who we are. If your parents were/are abusive, you can still consciously choose not to abuse others. Or if your parents were/are loving, you can choose this too. However you react, the main thing to know is that in this moment *you* decide how you want to live your life and what your values are. Use your history as knowledge that can help you become a better person. It's the best thing you could do.

If your parents didn't give you love, look to the place within yourself that feels like love, learn to truly take care of yourself, preferably holistically (including mind, body and spirit). This process can be difficult, and of course for many it is. If you have not been loved or nurtured how do you learn to be? Yet it is innate in the nature of humans to love; many would say it is our entire reason for being. However if we were not taught to love, we must teach ourselves how to.

It's important to remember that we do have control over the attitude and viewpoint we choose to adopt in any situation. It is totally up to us whether to view things with resentment or bitterness, regretting the past at the cost of the future or today, or whether we choose to *appreciate everything!* There are always choices we can make right now to improve our lives; all we need to do is be willing to make them.

Ideas and Solutions:

For those who desire it here are some basic steps on the journey to self-discovery:

- Look inward; what have you learnt about life and how does this shape your life? What morals has this developed in you? How much do you need to be right? Or what do you feel is wrong? Do you trust your instincts? Do you examine your true feelings? Do you act with compassion? Are you close with others who support you and your dreams? How can you develop your ability to love and to receive love? Be willing to get to know … yourself.

- Be open-minded; when you hear new information, do not disregard it. Be willing to search for truth that will enrich and broaden your understanding, not diminish it. Be open to different opportunities or ideas even if they make you feel uncomfortable initially. Usually what we resist the most helps to teach us the lessons we most need to learn. Sometimes the resistance might tell us what we don't want, or don't like, which can be very self-revealing; other times it can be that something's hit a nerve, and wherever that nerve is, it's a part of us that's seeking to be healed.

- The documentary *What the bleep do we know?* offers excellent insights into how our conditioning works amidst its extensive discussions on quantum theory.

- Trust your basic truths; the greatest truth of humankind is love. I believe true loving means having compassion for all life including our own, and acting accordingly.

Chapter 6 – Guilt

Once you have a basic understanding of yourself, you can then recognise the ways you may deny your own compassion and humanity—essentially meaning, caring about the world around us and our role in it. There are many ways we do this. One is to focus too much on ourselves, or on others. This self-focus may be boasting and big-noting ourselves, which makes it harder for us to see our place in the world. Feeling superior to others can only create feelings of separation from others. This can lead to people living in very isolated worlds, only comfortable with what they perceive as their 'own kind', and even then, isolated emotionally within their group. Arrogance and ego are always downfalls; there is no competition when we all have unique differences in our gene patterns, upbringings, skills, talents etc. The only person we can ever truly be better than is the person we were yesterday; we can never be 'better' than others because the playing field is never even.

The other way we suppress our humanity is by focusing on ourselves too much through self-doubt and insecurity, simply because it is selfish to be self-absorbed. Many people who suffer from this may be consumed with trying to help everyone around them to 'prove they're a good person' as a way to repair their low self-esteem and in most cases they themselves are running ragged. As soon as we unnecessarily put others' needs ahead of our own we are setting an unhealthy example. We are in effect saying, 'my needs don't matter', forgetting that we all essentially need the same things. Without understanding this truth we may find ourselves in a perpetual state of guilt.

A person suffering from guilt may blame themselves for 'not being perfect' yet attaining perfection through their all-critical eyes is near impossible. Still many may believe they are good people because 'at least they care'. They may believe they only feel guilty because they want to do the right thing, they just don't know how to successfully achieve it. They believe that if they try harder, they could absolve their guilt for good. They also believe that beating themselves up is 'ok' because 'at least they're not hurting others'. They believe it's alright to punish themselves for being 'bad', i.e. not perfect, and this somehow makes them 'good', because at least they're not arrogant or egotistical.

The problem with these people is that they are so sucked into their own inner dialogues that although they think they are helping others, in many cases they are only projecting their own needs.

They don't have the objective ability to see another individual's problem and what help they may actually need. They are so busy thinking, 'If I do this, that will make them feel better, it's what I'd want someone to do for me, so of course that'll make them happy' and so on. At no point does the guilt ridden person stop, observe and ask, 'What do they *actually* need?' Or even better, 'What do *I* actually need?'

There are many examples of this sort of projection: someone who really wants to change aspects of their life, starts encouraging their friends to do the same, whether or not it's appropriate for them; friends/partners/parents constantly pushing others to 'fulfil their dreams', get that 'job, mark, achievement', whilst not working on empowering themselves or fulfilling their own dreams; constantly offering things we ourselves want; criticising others for something we don't like about ourselves; doing favours for people so that we feel we've 'done something' or so 'we don't have to confront them'; the list goes on and on. When we do this we are simply deferring our own issues and often times we become way too embroiled in the affairs of others.

Can you see how easily we can project our desires by wanting everyone else to 'have it all'—or feeling resentful because we may assume they already do—when all the while we are denying ourselves?

If we want the people we love to become self-fulfilled and empowered, *we* must become self-fulfilled and empowered! In fact, if we are not leading by example, how can we expect our advice to be taken seriously? You cannot preach what you cannot do if you expect others to follow you.

I believe we are all projecting our desires or beliefs onto others to a greater or lesser degree, depending on our own level of self-awareness.

Therefore it is essential that we stop and ask ourselves: Are we offering this because we truly believe it is in the best interest of the other? Or is the offer based on our own needs, to be the giver? Offering everything all the time clearly demonstrates that it is about the givers own needs, because help will be offered even when it isn't appropriate. In certain situations the offer to help may actually agitate someone or 'get their back up'; it may make them feel powerless, or judged, as if we are saying 'you can't do it on your own'. Instead of helping others, we may actually undermine their confidence, or worse, encourage their dependency on us, creating a climate where the other may grow to feel incapable of doing things for themselves, rendering them powerless. Of course if the giver then becomes sick of giving that support, their withdrawal may upset the receiver even more; it must be done in the right way, by guiding that person to other support, most especially that which they can give themselves.

In reality we all need to solve our own problems because we each carry the unique knowledge of our own life. The answers we seek are already within us; external influences can only mirror or trigger recognition that is there to begin with, albeit dormant.

To truly help another is about being able to observe and assess what we believe the best help would be, even if this means not getting involved. In a real way we could relate this idea to good parenting or good teaching, and ultimately, to good relationships. When our child/student/human is doing a task, sometimes it's best not to offer help too quickly, so that they have a chance to experience solving the problem for themselves. Other times they may be shy to even attempt the task, or may become frustrated, and then it's important to step in and offer support to help them get through that particular block. To truly encourage and foster learning in our children/students/humans, we use a number of different strategies depending on the particular individual or situation. This is what loving actually is. We *don't* project our own needs and desires onto others; we appreciate and value theirs.

Some people can be guided to helping themselves; others need to figure it out on their own. Some people have blocks to accepting help, the best thing to do is to respect this and don't offer. Let them know you're there by being available, let them come to you when they're ready. If I feel drained after helping someone it means I've been trying too hard (projecting) or the caring is not being received, therefore it is negated. When I truly help another I am doing what's right for me, and that is the best respect I could give them, as helping others at my own expense is clearly hypocritical. Of course some situations require our help even if we are weak. Yet will and compassion can create miracles in times of greatest need. It is an important lesson to offer healing even if we cannot relate to the situation requiring it, because we all require love.

When you do what's right for you, you inspire others to do this too.

If it's not a good time for you to talk or act or help, say something! Be honest with others about your own needs, and if they don't want to oblige you, perhaps you can teach them to respect the needs of others. Giving in to other people's demands against your will can only create resentment. Helping them use you doesn't help them.

The best way to help anyone, especially if you allow other people to treat you badly, is to heal yourself to begin with. Just remember that for most humans, it doesn't feel good hurting people. Those who you may feel a victim of are very possibly tortured in the fact that their abuse literally denies them of your love. Allowing people to hurt you hurts them too.

I am not saying, do not be generous; on the contrary, be very generous, except in situations where your generosity is inhibiting another's growth! The essential need to those who are suffering is to know that someone cares. One must not only be there, but always encourage empowerment for all individuals.

****

On the subject of guilt, I must mention the consequential guilt felt by those who have hurt others. (The type of guilt I am describing above is more like 'hysterical guilt'; self-imposed by those who over worry or over do—even if that's not doing, i.e. too much apathy causing guilt. Interestingly enough, a lot of this guilt people feel most likely stems from the fact that they are not taking care of themselves properly; they may be feeling guilty because they are ignoring their *own* needs.) Guilt or conscience is like a behavioural recording system, telling us whether actions we have committed have caused pain to others (or ourselves!). Feelings of this nature can cause great grief, yet it is very important for these people to, if possible, really understand how they feel, learn from it, and work on coming to a place of healing.

If you are feeling guilty and would like to resolve it, take all avenues possible to forgive yourself, and do what you can to heal the situation with those you feel you've hurt. You could write a letter or write it all down; record your thoughts to help elucidate what your true feelings are. Allow yourself to talk to others about it if possible. You could call a free service to talk it out, like Lifeline, for example. In the process of seeking healing you will more than likely desire to seek atonement with all those involved.

Many people that feel they have hurt others tend to also feel very hurt and misunderstood by others. In many cases, they are hurting themselves more than anyone. Either way forgiveness allows one to move on.

On the subject of forgiveness, I offer you these words from Louise L Hay:

> Forgiveness means giving up, letting go. It has nothing to do with condoning behavior. It's just letting the whole thing go. We do not have to know HOW to forgive. All we need to do is to be WILLING to forgive. The Universe will take care of the *hows*.[74]

I believe that forgiveness comes from letting go of the resentment we may feel towards others and we can do this by taking care of ourselves properly. If we felt very hurt, we can choose to do all those things for ourselves that we may have felt others denied us; that very right of being cared for.

Remember each individual is the source of all love, compassion and understanding. These states of being

---

[74] Hay, p. 8. Hay offers a visualisation exercise for those who feel they may need to vent before getting to forgiveness, p. 71. I agree that anger must be expressed as safely as possible for some people before they can work on letting go of a painful memory. Hay offers some excellent exercises throughout her book, all of which can help dissolve anger. I offer some brief suggestions for clearing anger in here on pages 143 and 149-150 respectively.

reside in our very own hearts. They are the tools that bring peace into our own lives, which therefore brings peace into the lives of others.

It is very sad when we hurt those we love and find ourselves unwilling to compromise. In the difficult moments, decide what you really need to express to that person. If you truly love them, reach out to them even if it means swallowing your pride.

To see whether forgiveness is needed, we can send loving thoughts to people and note our resistance to doing so. We can wish everyone in our lives well, no matter what their journey is. Just thinking about all our relationships with peace and love can dramatically affect us for the better. Telling people how we really feel, without judging or blaming them, can bring much needed balance into all our relationships. Being honest with others proves that we *do* care about the relationship, because long suppressed feelings end up erupting and doing a lot more damage. This is why truth and love are synonymous. Once you remove your own resentment, all that's left is love.

> ... *I let go of a broken heart, I let go to an open heart*
> *I let go of my broken dreams, I let go to the mystery*
> *And I believe in the miracle, I believe in the spiritual*
> *I believe in the one above, I believe in the one I love*
> *Even when I've fallen down my heart says follow*
> *through and I take one step closer to you*[75]

****

---

[75] Michael Franti & Spearhead, *One Step Closer to You,* music album, Yell Fire!, Michael Franti, Boo Boo Wax, 2006.

And last but not least, there is the guilt involved with feeling that one has a 'wonderful life', with an overabundance of things, when so many others are missing out. Let's just look at the irony.

Yes, we live in an incredible country (in Australia, and other 1st World countries) where it's pretty easy to eat and fulfil our needs (aside from the underprivileged of course!). We run around feeling guilty for what we have, or not appreciating it.

But, we can *always* give money to the underprivileged if we have the dollars to spare; we can donate to charities and do volunteer work; we can encourage others to care about world poverty and discuss measures to address this within our individual powers; we can vote for governments that will at least look at these issues. There is so much we can do in our position. And we can appreciate everything that we have! I am telling you Free World, there is no point living in this incredible comfort (i.e. having access to food, water, employment, welfare, freedom of speech, etc.[76]) if we do not appreciate it. This is the key emotion to reaching inner peace on all levels. Appreciation is an expression of gratitude from our hearts for everything we do have and comes with a real knowledge that others don't have anywhere near the same as we may. We each need to do what we can to make sure there is a balance. Those of us that are comfortable are the ones we need to fight the most! Fight for humanity. Fight for the same for everybody. The discrepancies between 1st and 3rd World countries are utterly horrifying. We have excess and are

---

[76] Just think of how many humans have valiantly fought and still fight for these rights today.

therefore wasteful, whilst a miniscule amount of our excess could turn a life of futility into one of hope. Nothing makes any of us so special that we, the human race, don't all deserve the same things. We all deserve the bare minimum of luxury: food, water, air, shelter, love.

Can't you see the greater need? We are so bogged down with all our own inner guilt and dialogues that we are denying our power as healers and humanitarians. How do we help others when we can't even help ourselves? We, who have so much opportunity to focus on our growth, have a responsibility to do so! Those who are materialistic have a need for healing too. There are starving kids in the world, homeless people, war; do you really think we would allow governments to continue such oppression if we were healed ourselves? Dear Lord—or every living cell in the Universe! Can't you see Western society is set up in such a way so that we *do* just focus on ourselves? We get caught up in our own problems or our own selfishness. That—war, hunger, oppression—is in the 'too hard basket', it's 'just the way it is'; these are all the ways we deny our own power.

But don't you see we run the world? (According to Chomsky, world public opinion is the world's second superpower.[77]) Whether we work or not, we all spend money on the goods and services that keep our economy going. Can you see that without that labour, without us working for or consuming from the richest corporations, that they would go broke? Think of how often our government is influenced by the rich, and how often

---

[77] Chomsky, p. 10.

business interests and profit win out over basic human decency.

Imagine if we turned our product love into people love. Rather than buy new products, we would give money to those in need, to those who are hungry right now. Imagine if we all helped to alleviate suffering, instead of buying new cars and possessions. *How much satisfaction would that bring?*

You may think this all sounds far-fetched but I am just mentioning some of the ways we could make things better. The essential point is that we may not be able to even begin these discussions—about what we could do on a national and global level—until we are willing to become more humane ourselves as otherwise we'll continue wallowing (self-pity) and swallowing (consumerism). There is a bigger picture; it's called The World. An awful lot of people are suffering terribly, so the sooner we get over ourselves and all we don't have (when really we have an overabundance of our basic needs) the better it will be for everyone, including us.

Many feel guilty about having all this but what a waste of time! It is what we have, it is what is here. We can make our lives simpler whenever we want. We can reduce our own needs. There are plenty of people in Australia going without a lot of things right now; those that feel they have excess can pass some of it on to them.

Our appreciation levels are dependent on the way we view things. When I leave a tap running and know I need to save water it is not because Australia has an apparent 'water shortage' (although this situation has been worsening) it is because every drop I waste would be utter bliss for a person in a hot dusty desert in the middle of a civil war, or the like. I turn off that tap out of respect for all I have, and all others don't have.

We need this awareness in all aspects of our lives. It is this awareness and appreciation that will clear our minds for the work that could possibly be done. And I hope, as you read this, you don't believe that nothing can be done, because when you really look at it, when have we—as a collective 1st World—*ever really tried?*

The problem is we have all our necessities covered yet we spend little time working on our own honesty and our humanity and this is what makes us miserable! People in the 1st World need to fill their hearts with love and appreciation and then demonstrate this in their external world, guiding others to the same sense of peace; the kind that comes from simplicity, awareness and love. We must emanate this compassion until everyone is aware of the work that needs to be done. It is only when we have enough healing souls that we will start to vote in better politicians. Our humanity will give us the strength to change the political systems. Our efforts will greatly change our society for the better.

Our political systems should be made up of many sensible factors (not currently present), such as: recognition of others' views; negotiation; honest communication; and above all; humanity and compassion. At the moment, our own parliament seems to be a bloodthirsty rabble where every politician is dogged down by their rivals until their sense of morality is broken. In the end, they too may become a power hungry pawn for the prime minister. These types of politicians are all twisted up inside; they have lost great perspective of the greater good. They are so bogged down in political gains that the overall well-being of the masses has become irrelevant.

This is how prosperous governments allow people to starve; they are not even thinking about poverty and human suffering, they are only thinking about how to retain or increase their own power. Therefore we must encourage and support those in politics who have a genuine sense of social justice and honestly want to develop our systems for the better.

The fact is that the First World countries live off the Third World, (but remember my friends, it is all One World). We exploit those who can do little to protect themselves or their land. We take their resources for next to nothing, and not give *one iota of a damn* when those people can no longer feed themselves, or when their water systems are poisoned because some multi-billion dollar corporation didn't want to clean up properly. The fact that many living in Western society may be unaware of this is totally ironic when many products we buy are directly linked with these types of corporations.

In regards to your own appreciation, my advice is to look at your world with open eyes and really see it. We have way more than is necessary. We are throwing food out!! The scraps from our dinner plates would feed a village in Africa, or still be hot if we offered it to the hungry in our own cities. (And what is stopping any of us from making them fresh meals? Or supporting community food buses to feed the homeless?) We need to get over our materialistic desires and realise it's truly disgusting that we have *so* much when others have *so* little. This disgust is compounded when you look at all the petty little things we complain about.

Ideas and Solutions:

- Instead of complaining (if you do); appreciate everything!
- Reach out to those you love rather than pushing them away. If you cannot trust them with your vulnerability, try to see the vulnerability in them. Perhaps they are displaying theirs in a different way to you (for example, some people respond with anger when they feel vulnerable). If neither of you are growing, at least take the time to focus on your own growth.
- Relationships *can be* tricky. We are essentially combining our own inner reality with another's but if we understand that our own conditioning colours our view, it is much easier to diagnose problems in our interactions. This does take a certain amount of maturity; the act of being able to admit one's needs or negative behaviour during arguments or tense interactions means taking full responsibility for oneself. This doesn't mean we sugarcoat it if others behave badly, as we must be firm with any person who acts disrespectfully, but in understanding the fears, beliefs, hopes or failings in our own behaviour, it's much easier to understand these behaviours in others and therefore work towards more mutually empowering relationships.
- The West is currently embracing many paths to healing. Yet there is an argument going around

that this is merely more self-indulgence. Although this may be true for some, you will find that most, if not all, people that seek healing do so because they are suffering in some way. Healing is a way for people to see what that suffering is about and to heal by returning to wholeness. An important aspect to healing is to understand the truth; that we are *not* alone, *not* separate, but rather connected to *all* life. While we're on the subject though, one way to cure any self-indulgence is to play our own parts in creating peace; in our own hearts, in our own lives, in our own streets.

Chapter 7 – Distraction

They tellin' you to never worry 'bout the future
They tellin' you to never worry 'bout the torture
They tellin' you that you will never see the horror
Spend it all today and we will bill you tomorrow[78]

If guilt is one of the ways we deny our own humanity, distraction is possibly just as lethal.

How many days are you driven by purely external situations? From the moment you wake up it's a barrage of thoughts: Got to get to work, get the kids to school, get a haircut, see my friends, help my neighbour, walk my dog, etc.

Constantly thinking about how to pay the bills, how to get ahead, pay the mortgage, etc.

People seem to work so hard to get their 'dream life' (stereotypically a house, car, two kids and a dog) but when they get there they're working so hard to maintain all that. When do they get the time to actually enjoy it? The cost of mortgages and interest rates are only increasing. A standard house costs around half a million dollars now, which I don't believe is genuinely balanced with wage increases. But we basically need to be millionaires to own our own house comfortably without accruing a lifetime debt. Just look at what housing debt has done in America; 2 million people are about to have their homes foreclosed (many of them having been granted dubious loans) creating shockwaves on the

---

[78] Michael Franti & Spearhead, *Yell Fire!,* 2006.

stock market at 1st August 2007.[79] This is a good example of 'capitalism gone crazy' where businessmen are encouraged to increase their own profits (for instance in this case selling poxy debts to foreign investors) regardless of any ethical consequences.

And we are heading down America's road on many fronts. The standards of health, education and welfare in this country are rapidly diminishing yet the problems of homelessness, drug addiction, polarisation and violence are only increasing.

Then there are the HECS[80] debts (called HELP[81] now) that we accrue when we acquire those university degrees that will put us in a higher earning bracket. A generation ago there was no such cost. If your family is well-off and can support you in some ways, then you might be ok. If they can pay your fees you can save a lot of money on interest. It's ironic how often upfront payments are rewarded with lower interest rates; the poor can't afford to pay upfront and therefore accrue the most interest (it's the same as getting fined for not having enough money in your bank account). Too bad if there's no wealth in your family; it is much harder to create wealth from nothing than it is for a wealthy person to donate money.

As the divide between rich and poor deepens and with all the costs of living only increasing, it seems that people are working harder than ever but without seeing

---

[79] SBS, *Newshour,* television program (U.S.), Australia, 1 August 2007.
[80] Higher Education Contribution Scheme.
[81] Higher Education Loan Program.

the extra rewards. The ultimate cost for working people is stress. In this 'lucky country' there are more people breaking their backs—both literally and figuratively—trying to keep themselves afloat, than there are relaxed people able to take care of their own well-being and the well-being of others (like their family). The working life seems to take just the right amount of time so that people never quite get the chance to STOP. The ratio of 8 hours work, 8 hours sleep, 8 hours play, does not add up when you look at other factors such as travel and home maintenance, and most especially, child rearing! Play time is radically reduced in our modern lifestyle, and often the relaxation or play comes in the form of TV, movies, games or computers. Of course there are other great activities that I'm sure many enjoy, such as cultural events, outdoor activities, hobbies, sports and so on. But many hard working people don't seem to get the time to do any of this! It seems their main reward is that yearly holiday, which, like everything else in the modern world, costs money. The money people make is the same money they then spend; most of it goes to multi-billion dollar companies, such as real estate and utility companies, and to industries, such as the travel industry, or the movie industry. The money people earn just pays for *things* but you cannot buy peace or happiness or sanity; these are all states of being, or states of mind that emanate from within. Even if money helps us, it's our own attitudes that ultimately allows it to; our belief that it's needed to solve problems. Yes we need housing and the security that brings but so much of our money is spent on much more trivial things. So I just don't know if supporting this work/earn/buy capitalist system is in the best interest of human beings, for their happiness, health and well-being, or in the best interest of our societies as a whole.[82]

Yet, in comparison to poorer countries, we have got it great. It's just that people here do not seem to value it as much as they probably would if they experienced what working for a day in a Chinese factory was like. This would give them an excellent measure of standards; hence, appreciation. Yet the West is oppressed in its own ways. Many more people in Western countries die from stress and heart attacks and cancer than they do in poorer countries. These people die from lack of what we can buy at any pharmacy, or from what we were immunised against in Grade 1, or from lack of food. Yet many Westerners become ill because they work too hard and don't relax enough or they stress or worry or eat *too* much! There is truly great imbalance in the world; by balancing ourselves (one example is for those who feel they overspend to donate some money monthly to charity) we are mending the rift, and therefore able to restore the balance.

If people love their jobs, then hard work becomes good work, i.e. it may be hard but it's also good. This means they are fulfilling an inner need, not one demanded of them. If they are working merely to fulfil their obligations, they desperately need an outlet; something that satisfies not only their obligations but also their inner aspirations. To constantly work to keep everything going is to deny existence from moment to moment. We all need peace, which can come from knowing that what we do, we do because we truly want to. Much is gained

---

[82] If you are interested in alternatives check out The Venus Project in *Zeitgeist,* 2nd movie.

from pursuing the things we most love.

We have a choice. We may think our kids need wealth, for their education and to give them a proper life, but all the wealth in the world won't spiritually fulfil our children. The best thing we can do is observe what works best for them. This in turn, will be what's best for us; knowing they are doing what they love the most. Remember children can be extremely resilient and live on very little. As long as they have our understanding and our respect, I believe they will find ways to reach their own goals. Of course we must guide and provide structure. We all need 'training wheels' before we can learn to ride a bike on our own. It's important we teach our kids to be open-minded and flexible thinkers, so that they can learn to handle a number of situations, and continue the learning process in their own lives. And we must also allow ourselves to learn from them, each an incredible and unique individual. But no matter what else we teach our young, we must teach them how to feel good about themselves, not through competition or comparisons with others, but through teaching them to care for themselves; helping them to learn to recognise and understand their own values and abilities.[83]

It's hard for our young not to get caught up in all the advertising. Kids can be cruel to their peers in regards to the 'haves' and 'have-nots'. But loving them well, rather than buying endless products, is always your best option.

---

[83] Louise L Hay is doing some wonderful work in this area. I highly recommend you check out the books she has written for children and young people.

If you need to make time for self-healing, or to follow a dream, do not feel that this will be detrimental to your children's well-being. In fact, by truly taking care of yourself—even if this means time away from them—so long as you have the right intentions, you may actually be teaching them the greatest values possible. And they will be rewarded with a more centred, healthy and loving parent.

So; let's stop distracting ourselves with this insurmountable pressure we have placed upon our own shoulders by all we 'have to do'. Let's break it down to what we need to do, that which is best for our loved ones and ourselves. Really, all you need, and they need, is love.

Please remember that if you are stressed out or unhappy whilst trying to raise these kids, they will sense that on some level and probably become very stressed themselves. Just be honest with them about why you do what you do, because they may well rather be poor than grow up with the strain and stress that comes from living with an overworked parent or parents.

I completely understand that you need to feed and shelter your family, but this does not mean that in your spare time you couldn't read a nurturing book, or be creative. Many hard working parents start new ventures that breaks the monotony of the everyday and opens up other avenues for earning money. Yet the greatest things in this life are free, and no matter how rich or poor you are, the one thing human beings need to survive, to live (aside from food, water, shelter) is love from the people around them. If you have been terribly hurt, you somehow need to change the pattern where you continue to be hurt. But I will go into that in more depth later.

Please note: When I talk about fulfilling your needs, I am not talking about buying a wide screen TV (unless you *really* want to). I'm talking about our need to be at peace with what we are doing. An awful lot of people spend an awful lot of time being miserable in their job or life. I believe that when you find inner peace in your own life, in your own self, you will readily see solutions that will enrich you and the lives of those around you. When you're in a 'bad mood' you affect all those around you negatively. When you are happy, it is only natural that you have the power to affect others positively.

Ideas and Solutions:

- Put down your heavy burdens, even if just for a moment, take a deep breath and let it all go. Know that in this current moment just by changing your thinking or your perspective, you can change what is not working for you.
- Explore any or all methods of healing that you are drawn to.
- Take the chance to explore a dream you may not have followed. We generally create the most prosperity by doing what we are truly drawn to and what makes us truly happy.
- If you are materialistic, try encouraging Australian businesses to offer jobs to the Indigenous or homeless here rather than exploiting foreign workers.

Chapter 8 – Television

"Big brother is watching you."[84]

How many hours has the machine engulfed you? Oh I know some of it can be great. The mental 'break' can be wonderful after a stressful day, the 'time out'. There are many positive aspects of TV: the knowledge that one can acquire through watching documentaries; the insights that may occur whilst viewing; the connections that can form through community stations; the health benefits of laughter through comedy programs; the enjoyment one can experience from music programs. All these types of benefits are likely to be utilised by the sound minded. But how many people are? And how addictive is it for some? How often is it turned off in lieu of healthier activities, say, like reading, exercising, resting, meditating, relaxing, etc.? And how often do people question its negative aspects? Like the fact that television induces apathy.

When we sit passively watching television, it sets in. It becomes harder and harder to get up or to do something else; it's just easier to stay in TV world and keep watching. All the influx of images shuts down our ability for visualisation. We can't imagine what something looks like, when we're looking at it. It is completely different to reading books, because unless one has seen a movie of that book, what is visualised derives purely from one's own imagination.

It's the same as with our dreams. We cannot say that

---

[84] Orwell, *1984*, p. 3.

what we see in our mind's eye is not completely unique to each individual human being. And there must be a reason for that. We each have our own originality; it is innate.

Yet the American TV shows that have become so popular in Australia are aired to millions of viewers in America and around the world, and there is nothing original about it. The prolific increase in violence and sex is certainly not an original thought, quite obviously. It is of course about the ratings (money) and many viewers are sucked in; all the while the wealthy media moguls continue to dictate what we view at all.

If only the general public questioned the nature of our commercial media, and knew the intentions of those who govern it. For example, how many who have control over what is aired support the Iraq War? Why is violence used to subjugate the masses, with those purporting it ultimately making money out of misery? How is deadening our senses going to help us to evolve? Obviously, our mental, spiritual, emotional and physical health is not on the agenda. Currently, post Howard's 'free-trade' deal with the U.S., there is little room or funding for independent filmmaking in Australia. Our programs are overwhelmingly American now and the influence is far-reaching. Even Aussie shows like *Neighbours* have been compromised, changing their 'white picket fence' image to one where stalking, blackmail, adultery and even murder are becoming commonplace themes. *Idol, Survivor, Wheel of fortune, Top model*—the shows that have not originated from or are influenced by American TV are few and far between.

Most, if not all, of commercial TV is designed to influence our ideas, from what we wear, to what we buy, to what we watch, to what we eat, to how we think and feel. The effect this has on us and in the weak-minded (people who do not actively pursue learning and growth) can be powerful; it can completely influence our daily lives. Just think about the people you may have heard say: 'Those bloody Iraqi terrorists'. How much *Dateline* do you think they've watched? Some people believe that what they hear on the commercial stations is true. In many cases a great deal of what you hear may be a one-sided view; remember those media moguls have their own agendas and often work closely with government in delivering their mutually beneficial 'party lines'. To give an example of how this may manifest on a station influenced in this way, let's take a discussion on a current affairs program, or morning show, say, where the interviewer (station) is pro the Iraq War. At first the interviewer may seem like they are on the side of the anti-war commentator (usually someone who is closer to sitting on the fence than anti-war), to give the appearance that both sides will be represented, only to then try to discredit their views and give longer air-time to an absolute nut that will justify crimes against humanity under the guise of attempting to 'save' humanity. This is even more so the case in America. Out of 800 journalists sent to Iraq to report on the U.S. invasion, only 6 didn't support the war![85] But these insidious tactics to control information works; many people swallow the lies and will 'hate the enemy' dutifully. (See Orwell's *1984*.)

---

[85] Schechter, 2004.

Television does not ask us what we think; it tells us what we should be thinking and how we should be acting. Not only do many swallow up the news propaganda, directing their thinking to 'what's important right now', they faithfully follow it. Do you remember the Boxing Day tsunami? Yes, that was a terrible catastrophe, but it covered the news stories so prolifically that when it was quietly announced that the U.S. and Australia *knew* there were no Weapons of Mass Destruction *before* invading Iraq, no one seemed to notice. (They are known to have been destroyed after the Gulf War.[86]) Well done again, Howard government. In this case, the commercial news directed our thinking so that our leaders could get away with murder. It's that simple.

> Recognition that control of opinion is the foundation of government, from the most despotic to the most free, goes back at least to David Hume, but a qualification should be added. It is far more important in the more free societies, where obedience cannot be maintained by the lash. It is only natural that the modern institutions of thought control ... should have originated in the most free societies. Britain pioneered with its Ministry of Information, which undertook "to direct the thought of most of the world."[87]

When global environmental crises occur, leaving behind many victims, the richer countries rally their citizens to donate all they can, yet human crises occur every day due to war, poverty and disease, but there are no rallies

---

[86] Schechter, 2004. Mohammed Al-Douri, Former Iraqi UN ambassador gives sound reasons as to the truth of this.

[87] Chomsky, pp. 7-8.

to demand the world pool its resources to solve this problem. We are trained to respond only to those crises we are told to, and this deliberate measure of the worth of human beings is nothing less than moral subjugation. Both massively publicised and non-publicised crises deserve an equal response.

There are many ways to divert people away from the truth of this indoctrination, and ultimately from their own humanity. Sell them violence, sensationalise it. Make them think they want it. Here we turn to the subject of modern crime shows. In the 1980s *Murder she wrote* and *Columbo* were popular murder mystery programs. In most episodes the clues discovered by the protagonist typically came in the form of a button found on the floor, or via a character's suspicious behaviour. Nowadays, the clues are found in the form of blood at the crime scene, DNA, and what you find examining corpses. I remember one of the early ads for *Crime Scene Investigation* (*C.S.I.*) displayed a dictionary meaning of the word necrophilia, and then cut to the supposed offender of this crime who said something extremely disconcerting to justify it.[88] All *C.S.I.* ads are like this by nature, designed to shock and enthral. The one full episode I tolerated for research purposes (chosen at random) told the story of a 15 year old boy who had been mutilated and murdered (they showed his 'body'), the main suspect being another 15 year old boy

---

[88] The supposed perpetrator implied something like, 'she didn't say yes' so was justifying rape by taking her consent out of the picture. One can only hope our own fight for humanitarian ethics will render subject matters like these unconsciously by both TV producers and the morally subdued masses that apparently 'like' them.

who played fighting games with the victim, which were posted live on the Internet. This is just one example. You can't tell me this is healthy viewing for any human.

How can it be good that crime shows are so much more violent, more vile and sick than they have ever been? Just as horror films are increasingly trying to push our mental, psychological, and moral boundaries. How are shows like *Crime Scene Investigation, Waking the Dead, Cold Case, Bones,* (the list goes on and on), going to help my soul in any way at all? How can that possibly be good? People say, 'it's not real, it's not real', and to them I say, 'well, you're looking at it aren't ya? Those images and words are still seeping into your brain, and *that's* real'. Can you imagine showing these brutal shows to a 7 year old child that has never watched TV? Can you imagine the reaction they would have? There is an innocent child in all of us that feels that way if we watch these shows. Many teenagers and young children are still up at 8.30pm when *C.S.I.* airs.

Do you know how much simulated death and murder we see on TV? Can you even comprehend it? We are getting hammered with fear and hate and rage and we don't even realise it anymore.[89]

The indoctrination of thought in society through the use

---

[89] For those of you who are thinking, 'hey if this writer doesn't like what's on TV they should stop watching it!' my response to this is that as someone who is passionate about humanity I have a great interest in what is being shown and sold to the majority of people.

of television violence goes back to its earliest roots, most prominently manifesting in the propaganda films used during World War II. Post World War II, John Wayne and Clint Eastwood films are some examples of the gun clad hero who shoots and kills his way through obstacles and both acted as the symbolic soldiers of their day. Arnold Schwarzenegger films later continued this trend, indoctrinating yet another generation of young men with the belief that absolutely brutal violence is not only acceptable, but desirable.

Television can induce emotional responses from the viewer. But, that's why we watch it, isn't it? Watch a sad movie; have a good cry. Watch a thriller; experience excitement. Watch a comedy; laugh. TV can induce emotions but how are they invoked? TV producers know that when certain music is played with accompanying storylines filled with tension and release, that an emotional effect will usually be experienced by the viewer. They know *exactly* how we react as humans; understanding psychology is the fundamental premise on which advertisers and TV producers are able to sell their products at all. Using methods of psychology to manipulate us *is* unquestionably a mild, and often not so mild, form of brainwashing.

It is a very specific policy of the powers that be for television to manipulate our emotions to its pre-set intention. Does this somehow box our emotion, so that we may feel less emotional in our everyday lives? Have you ever heard someone say they only cry when watching a sad movie? Do you preserve *your* emotion for the TV or cinema? I don't need to see an ad about starving Africans to feel compassion for their situation; I already do by being aware of it. If we need an ad to remind us, doesn't that show how far removed we are from our own humanity? Even worse, they throw those ads at us so much that in the end we may just want to *change the channel!* And please research these charities that you are donating to, if you are. Ask where the money goes and try to discern which ones do the most practical good. There are some charities that believe one must convert to Christianity to be truly rewarded, to receive entitlement; a true charity does not judge its recipients. Many of the American Christian evangelical shows that are trying to convert you, and indeed *are* converting those stricken with disease and poverty; are extremely wealthy and extremely fundamentalist, so avoid donating to them at all costs. However there are many genuine charities that are in desperate need of support and which don't enforce their beliefs onto others; donate to them if you have a means to.[90]

There are many ways of indoctrinating free societies through the use of TV, and I turn to some of these now. Commercial current affairs programs are a good first example; topics covered predominantly include fashion, boob implants and scandal, inviting us to judge, to gossip and to endlessly worry about our appearance. Commercial news is even worse. They are only increasing in their sensationalism of violence, latching on (or should I say leeching on?) to anything they can get their hands on; now they even have their own ads. This is yet another extremely obvious form of inviting us to indulge in depravity; 'advertising' real crime and death. Why do we gasp in horror at the news stories about serial killers or isolated murders, but not blink an

---

[90] The non-profit charity Orphfund is an excellent example: www.orphfund.org

eye when our own government continues to support mass murder???

Plus there is the increase in anatomy shows. These first aired late at night on SBS, but now have spread like a virus to the other stations. I believe it is completely natural and healthy that many who have lived and who live today have strong feelings of sacredness for the human body and understand the right of physical privacy required by an individual. Now I know the bodies that have been used on these shows are people who consented to this before death. I also know that students of medicine and related vocations must do this type of work so that they can gain experience and knowledge in working with the human body. I don't particularly like it, but I very much appreciate the benefits and contributions made for the improvement of modern medicine, and all the lives that has saved. There are also medical programs that show operational procedures which are increasing in number. But, is everyone in society, or the people who watch these anatomy shows, going to be a doctor or working in a profession where the knowledge will be practiced? No! I do not believe this sort of programming is fit for the general populace. Yes, it is interesting; people can learn and be fascinated. It will also desensitise them to looking at something, most of us would deem, visually horrific. Unless it is for the purposes of knowledge, and practising knowledge, I see no joy in it. If people are really that curious then watching a video at the local library or hiring a DVD is something they'll pursue, but airing it to everyone may raise issues for many people. Each to their own, they say, but there are many in society who I definitely would *not* want to see these images: children, those with pathological disturbance, the elderly, and all those who have their own reasons for feeling sensitive about these issues. Taking that particular aspect—the dissection/autopsy of bodies—that originated for 'entertainment' by shows like the fictional *C.S.I.,* and then *doing it for real* seems rather disturbing if you ask me.

Remember most of our young just accept the brutality of today's TV. They have had images of sex and violence thrust upon them long before they could understand what they mean. It is not the sane and the just minded that we need to worry about, it is the easily influenced. The more we stray from a world where intelligence is valued, the stronger this influence becomes.

But it's true to a certain degree, if we are in control of our lives, that we choose what enters it. Personally I choose documentaries; channels ABC, SBS[91] and selected programs on Channel 31 (such as *Conversations with Robyn, Theories of Everything, Slow TV, Big Ideas,* etc.); political and social satire; fantasy; shows that expand your mind. I never choose to watch shows that sensationalise murder. Such terrible things occur in actual life; they can bring no joy, no understanding, and to watch shows about them can only create a quiet sense of malice.

I just don't understand how a fellow human can be shocked by a murder report on the news and then sit

---

[91] SBS are strong in terms of world news coverage and I am grateful for this, yet their choice of some foreign films is questionable at best, the most gruesome crossing lines that devalue humanity as much as *C.S.I.* at their worst.

down and for entertainment watch *Sensing Murder*. Yet human beings are *fed* these shows and human beings *eat* them. The ads for these shows, like *C.S.I.,* use voice-overs with that over exaggerated tone, declaring, 'This is exciting, this is hot, the most watched show in the U.S.', which may as well say, 'You can see hot dead bodies been cut up and investigated by us', but usually says, 'See tonight, a young beautiful girl is murdered. Who did it? Can *you* find the killer?' They sell it to you by instilling the idea that you already want it.

If watching these depraved shows is what the masses want, then it is tragic that human beings have turned out this way, or maybe they've never changed. The primal thirsts of lust and violence, that civilised living was meant to cure, are being thrust in our faces as if things never changed.

Just look at the sex ads 'streaming straight from the U.S.' (these are hard to avoid if you channel flick past midnight). They are growing ever more explicit, in fact, there is little left to show. One must ask oneself how many women do this *only* for the money (as oppose to wanting to). In America the costs of attending college are high; a low wage job doesn't cut it when you consider health care costs too. If without financial support from their families, taking off their clothes becomes a necessity for many. So the 'hot hot' girls that the advertising producers 'sex up' are more than likely girls struggling to pay for their basic commodities. To a great extent this also holds true for women in Australia and in many other countries.

We must ask ourselves why the people who control our media want us to be saturated with sexual imagery and violence. Perhaps some well thought-out plan to lead people to Christianity? When people roll around in the gutters of their base instincts they may at some point want to seek salvation; many 'born-again' Christians have sin-filled histories. Or is it just a way to keep the masses distracted so that those in power are able to control things as they like, ultimately steering the opinions of the masses? Or is it that with all the assaults of simulated sex and brutal violence in the media that people get to the point where they 'just don't care' obviously subjugating their humanity? Either way, when we live in our lower regions—where desire overrules reason—most of our time is spent seeking gratification, therefore limiting our use of the higher regions, where we can experience mental and emotional clarity. These basic urges are all well and good if we consider the human to be as any other animal; needing to breed and protect its own plot and all that, but not so suitable now in the 21st century where those living in comfort ignore those who are dying, not through need but through greed and stupidity, and when the planet itself could end because of these abominable traits. No animal is as stupid as that.

How well has the American film/TV industry programmed viewers in the world to accept simulated violence? We watch voyeuristically in the comfort of our own homes, calling all of our watching 'entertainment'. Because quite obviously if we ever found ourselves in a situation of real violence we would certainly not be enjoying it (perhaps some do). But do we believe it's 'ok' for the 'American hero' to brutally slaughter many people, because he is the 'good guy'? Think of any American action movie; the 'good guy' gets away with mass murder, because he is saving the 'good people', or because someone killed 'his people'.

There is almost always a 'pretty' girl involved who either needs protecting from the 'bad guys' and is often threatened with sexual violence.[92]

In a society where sexism, violence and sexual assault against women are still common occurrences, is it not possible that the media has a firm hand in this? Mass media is known to influence the masses to a certain degree otherwise it wouldn't be used for that purpose! (And guess what? Most of the people who control the mass media are men!) The good guy/bad guy scenario is imprinted everywhere we go, and not just on TV. Whole wars are started by America with these attitudes. But would the good guys really kill the bad guys? Wouldn't they prefer to heal them? Would a good guy become a murderer in the name of good? Perhaps he would if it was the only way to save another human's life, but other than that, it just doesn't work that way.

Think about this: If your heartstrings vibrate for the 'missing persons' and the 'victims' on these fictional shows, is it possible that this takes up the emotional space where caring for the world is meant to go? When crises are resolved, do you feel a sense of satisfaction? Does the typical plot line of the typical Hollywood action movie make you feel you have conquered the world, that *you* are the hero? Just by sitting on the lounge room couch, just by watching? But what if you need that energy to be the hero in your own life?

---

[92] In the last decade there has been an increase in 'women heroes'; same story, different sex. But you will notice that the males in the supporting roles are never threatened with violence or sexual assault to the degree that women often are when supporting a male lead character.

Television has many insidious tentacles. It seeps into our lives and saturates our minds. It can be very addictive and persuasive. It gets scarier when they start mixing fantasy with reality, like when *Law and Order* had a special on Iraq and Saddam (I saw the ad). I mean, is this some kind of a joke? They are using their fantastic crime shows to spread the propaganda of the American government. And now they're trying to convince the masses that they don't just want the made-up shows, portrayed with contrived realism, *they want the real thing!* Ever increasing are shows like *Real Life Crime, Missing Persons Unit,* and nothing shows the true cross-over from fantasy to reality better than in shows such as *Crime Investigation Australia,* (graphically documenting the most brutal murders in Australian history), and *True C.S.I.* (U.S.). The 10 seconds I saw of a *True C.S.I.* episode showed the bodies of naked murdered teenagers no older than 14 and in this case where the female victim had been sexually assaulted. This is how far American TV has gone in indoctrinating us to accept true violence, and Australia is playing the sheep every step of the way.

The graphic realism of ads for violent games is growing daily, the merging of fantasy and reality well and truly entrenched, even though we *know* these images are so close to the real violence that is actually committed against real people in various regions in the real world, we are so used to it by now that it flies past our moral radar. In Western societies real violence seems to be increasing, at least one would assume this from watching the news (remember fearful societies tend to be the most obedient and many 'buy into' the fear). Yet unfortunately this does not make the increase in real violence any less true, but in fact feeds it, so we must

103

ask ourselves, how much of this increase *is* due to the continual themes of bloodshed we view on TV? Of course, the majority of people in society do not commit crimes because of something they saw on the news or on a crime show. But those in the minorities; how may they have been influenced? The human imagination is seemingly limitless; the most heinous ideas are sold to us again and again as the number one entertainment factor.

The trend of teenagers and even primary school children filming school fights and posting them on the web is growing constantly, yet isn't this violent behaviour completely endorsed by what these kids see on TV every night? The sale of violence is predominant throughout the media, so of course many youth consider it 'cool'. But what happens to these kids as they grow older? In these capitalist societies many feel left behind and for some crime can be a way to get attention; indeed the most shocking crimes scream at us from the media constantly. When terms like 'brutally murdered', 'raped', 'dead', etc., are constantly hammering at us, the terms themselves begin to lose meaning. We can become completely desensitised to their usage.[93] Yet one must remember there are always real human beings connected to these stories, to whom these terms used

---

[93] The mobile phone ad selling the ring tone 'dead terrorist' is a perfect example of this, completely disrespecting the many who have lost lives in suicide attacks, largely committed in response to the subversive terrorist campaigns committed *by* the West. Desensitising us to the words 'dead' and 'terrorist' is terribly convenient when we understand that this is a deliberate subjugation of our morality, *especially* considering the West's barbaric practices committed against people in the name of the 'war on terror'.

blatantly and insensitively would be deeply offensive; to constantly use this language, to 'sell' these crimes, and for the populace to accept it or even like it, is, to say the very least, absolutely disrespectful to human life.

I just find it utterly insane that the world is saturated with countless murder shows, both real and fictional, and people all over the world sit on their arses and watch them, while the governments of those same people wilfully destroy *masses* upon *masses* of innocent human beings in even more gruesome ways. If one wants to see brutality and murder, all one has to do is to watch SBS World News, or doco's on the fascist regimes of the world, or any doco that legitimately analyses the events of the aforementioned wars. Because while we're trying to figure out 'who done it' on some *absolutely bullshit show,* our own leaders are committing far more heinous crimes that go completely unnoticed! Sometimes they show us these crimes (Abu Grahib pictures) and they *still* go unnoticed, slipping into our desensitised 'there's nothing I can do about it', basket. Doesn't anybody else see the irony of this? Does anyone else see the horror?

Wake Up World, please, Wake Up World.

Ideas and Solutions:

- Read George Orwell's *1984*. The implications of this book are only becoming more relevant in our current societal set-up.
- Turn off the TV! Read or muse instead.
- Write to the Free TV body and to the communications Minister if you feel there is any

truth in my observations. Keep in mind that the Free TV ads began shortly after the use of sex and violence on TV in Australia increased dramatically (post the free-trade agreement). By giving people the option, some may feel they don't need to express their concerns; they believe that others will do that for them. In many cases to effect change, that 'other' person needs to be you (me).

- During the Vietnam War, footage of the atrocities was shown on TV and many people reacted to the images. They felt that it was valuable to bear witness to the truth of those atrocities, and seeing what was actually happening gave them impetus on which to act (remember the images of children exposed to Napalm used by the U.S. and allies). I have heard people of that era say, 'We knew that society wouldn't stand for it'. Yet, just 40 years later, the same kind of images are shown on TV without penetrating the most part of society. I know this because Howard was voted back in. It is devastating that our senses are now so dulled that horrific images of people suffering through these wars that we actively support does not create a prominent backlash in our societies as it did back then; the nature of human suffering hasn't changed, only our lack of response to it.

- Our young are so exposed to, and influenced by, TV. It is essential that we encourage them to be free, compassionate and discerning thinkers.

Chapter 9 – Advertising

Did you ever get the feeling that you're not good enough, or that you don't have enough? Can you imagine in your life just how much you have consumed and how much you have been consumed? How many times have you felt in lack, in some way or form, because of all that seems expected in this commercial world?

Did you ever wonder if you would feel any of these things if you grew up in the bush, in a natural environment? Or if you were a cave man, a hippie, or a humanitarian?

Do you understand that you may have actually been brainwashed?

Do you understand that beauty is in the eye of the beholder?

Do you understand that all human beings, no matter what their figure or disfigurement, or what they are wearing, are divine and beautiful beings? How, you ask? Why?

Because we all have a heart and mind; we have the power to care for others! If you are a person who has cared for anyone you have already raised the level of peace in this world no matter how ugly you think you are. Please remember that. In relation to the examples above: a cave man doesn't care how he looks; a genuine hippie believes in World Peace and isn't self-conscious; a humanitarian experiences inner peace knowing they are doing all they can. Yet in modern society many people do not feel an inner sense of peace, they are unhappy with themselves and/or with others. Many people may believe and think: "I'm Not Good Enough!"[94]

But who are they trying to be good enough for?

These are my thoughts for those of you who feel this way: Your opinion of yourself has far more weight than anything others could do or say. If you value yourself, criticism can be listened to and even welcomed. If you don't, then you may feel regularly criticised, when others are only making an observation or expressing their own feelings. But at the end of the day, do you really think all the people you encountered are staring at their ceilings thinking about how you looked or acted? They are locked inside their own heads too, and possibly *just* as insecure as you.

If you feel insecure about yourself and/or your looks, your perception of how others see you may be totally clouded by your own self-judgments. If you didn't judge yourself so harshly, you would realise that how you look just isn't important, especially in relation to those who love you.

Your external world is a reflection of your inner thoughts. If you are judging yourself, you will feel judged by others. If you feel 'ugly' you will find people to mirror this belief. If you feel 'fat' you will be traumatised by pictures of 'beautiful thin women'—not

[94] Hay, p. 6. Louise L Hay, a healer of many decades, states that: "The Innermost Belief for Everyone I Have Worked with Is Always, "I'm Not Good Enough!"."

that all women aren't exposed to this and there are many thin women that feel they should still lose more weight. Please understand that these 'beautiful thin women' you see in the media are suffering just as much as you. They go to incredible lengths to maintain that image. Many of the models you see on magazine covers are anorexic or bulimic. They cannot enjoy real food or nourishment, because to maintain their semi-skeleton look they have to regularly starve themselves. Would you rather go hungry all the time than to be well fed? Do you want the pressure of the lights and the constant schedules just so you can feel beautiful? Do you see how ridiculously far you would have to go to look like one of those models? Is it worth it?

Do you agree that being healthy, no matter what your body size, is the most important thing?

If you don't, then you are invalidating the fact that you are human. Your body is like a car that needs maintenance. Just as a car will break down without water and petrol, if you do not give your body what it needs, it too will stop running just as if it were a machine. This is true for all of us. Yet the stamina we humans have to fill our bodies with toxins, survive and even regenerate healthy cells is quite extraordinary too. But the fact is we all do look very different.

Some women suffer from feeling they have 'too small or large' breasts, some men from feeling they have 'too small or large' genitalia[95] and both sexes from thinking

---

[95] Some may laugh and say 'all men want big sexual organs' when the reality is many that do may have difficulty in their sex life as this makes intercourse too painful for the other.

they are 'too fat' (or too thin in some cases). But the thing is, human beings find different things attractive, and there are people in the world that would find you attractive exactly how you are right now. Aside from this, people will love you for who you are, regardless of external factors. But if you cannot accept your external appearance, then it is clear to me that you need to find inner peace.

How we feel is a lot more important than how we look.

Just think about that for a minute. Doesn't that mean that even if we were acne prone or overweight people, if we felt good being alive that it just doesn't matter?

What do *you* think?

If you do believe 'I am fat and ugly' and are unwilling to take care of yourself lovingly regardless of how you look, then I guess you are focusing all your energy on losing the weight, right? But if all the diets in the world won't work, can't you just eat as healthily as you can and accept yourself the way you are?[96] You still have so much to offer the world just by being in your position. You could help others try to come to terms with their body size, if no amount of treatments has helped them. Even better, you could decide that you want to find inner peace and seek healing regardless of your looks and encourage others to do the same.

---

[96] Of course there are other issues here. For example an overweight person may not feel good physically, which then feeds the negative feelings and bad eating habits. Still, feelings of self-worth need to be cultivated to break this cycle.

Can't you see it's just a distraction from your life's calling?

We are not put here on earth to focus only on ourselves, and our external selves at that, for one whole lifetime! How utterly insane! Can't you see that if overweight or 'ugly' people (remember beauty is in the eye of the beholder) were glorified on the screen and in all advertisements, that it would be the thin or 'pretty' people feeling ugly? Can't you see that it's brainwashing endorsed by the people who control the world? It's a set-up, and you're the victim. Can you see that as long as you feel bad or sorry for yourself or harbour self-hatred that you cannot commit to your own healing and that of the world? Can you see that if you find inner peace you would help the world by being one less person staring at their face and body and feeling terrible about themselves?

Imagine what the hypothetical aliens would think if they observed us: 'Strange species, these humans. All the other life forms like rabbits, hippopotamuses, and bugs, etc., seem perfectly capable of surviving without analysing and hating their bodies every second of the day. Humans obviously come in a variety of shapes and sizes, yet they seem to be the only species hung up on it.'

And just how hung up are we?

We have entered what I call The Plastic Age.

You see, the problem with all this focus on our external selves is that people are becoming less real. As we have been convinced that appearance *is* important, we have

111

forgotten that what's on the inside is important too. This is a basic flaw in our current state of existence. But many have gauged that if they don't feel good on the inside, the outside may suffer too, so they then seek more remedial treatments, such as having regular massages. Then we start to approach the subject of healing and relaxation. Relaxation *is* the miracle cure.

> Living with mind and body relaxed is our natural state, our birthright - it is only the pace of our lives that has made us forget. Those who retain the art possess the key to good health, vitality and peace of mind, for relaxation is a tonic for the whole being, liberating vast resources of energy.[97]

All the healers of the world know this, and we all have the potential to be healers. Reiki, Tai Chi, Yoga, to name a few; these are some of the healing systems that understand the universal energy that exists in every living cell. If our own cells are relaxed they can reach their fullest capacities to heal our bodies; kind of like hitting the reset button, restoring us to wholeness. If an overweight person practised Tai Chi regularly they would increase their relaxation levels, therefore releasing the stress from their body, which would probably even allow them to lose weight.

Healing the inner self is the pathway to inner peace.

If we find this to be true in our lives we begin to transcend all those things we used to think mattered, like external appearance.

---

[97] L Lidell, with Narayani and Giris Rabinovitch, *The book of Yoga,* Great Britain, 1983, p. 23.

If you consider yourself a horrible sight, what if you were nursing the sick or dying? Can you see that through your own humanity, you could save yourself?

Looks is plastic. Looks is shallow. Looks is the shell. It is the beating heart and the throbbing soul that will lead you to your greatest good. Listen to what your instincts say.

You have to know that how a person looks has no bearing or relevance on how beautiful that person could be.

Try to look deeper into the surrounding society that has caused you to feel all this pain about your looks. Fast food industries have spread like a virus throughout the world and during the same time obesity has increased prolifically. But the thing is, people out there are making billions of dollars, whether it's McDonalds or the 'slimming' industry. Either way they both win, but you lose (unless the slimming programs actually work for you).

The power hungry men of the world want you to feel fat and ugly. Want you to feel self-conscious. Because as long as you're spending time consumed with thinking about it, as long as you are spending a lot of money 'trying to fix yourself', as long as you are ruled by self-hatred and guilt, they can continue destroying the world while you lock yourself inside your house staring at a mirror.

I hope with all my being that you can hear what I am saying. There are more important issues at hand. Our own humanity is being destroyed! We are becoming the plastic people. Can't you see where all this is leading? Imagine the future of our current path. More and more women replacing their own breasts, removing their natural body fat and inserting plastic!! The implications right now are women feeling they are rejects of society if they don't reach a certain breast size. This situation is growing more ludicrous by the day, as ever more billions are spent collectively on plastic surgery. A good example of this beauty hypocrisy is that even though report after report shows that tanning salons can cause skin cancer they still operate unquestioned at many beauty shops; this essentially implies that being 'beautiful' is more important than being alive! But how can that be?!

Another huge pressure on women is hair removal. Every hair except that on the head must be religiously removed. If a woman exposes underarm or leg hair in public, they are often stereotypically viewed as a 'feral', a 'hippie', or the classic one, 'a lesbian'. Society does not sell them as sexy, anywhere in our society, ever.[98] Women cannot even enjoy their own natural human bodies without being judged like this! But you know what? *Hair grows naturally.* Just look at the explosion of beauty salons providing Triple X waxing (the removal of all genital hair). Women are having this done increasingly; apparently many men (and women) see it as 'sexy'. But, isn't genital hair a sign of a woman coming *into* her sexuality?? Let's face it. The fact is the only women who naturally have no genital hair are girls who are still children, and the very elderly. And for many very humane reasons we do not consider

---

[98] This is not to say that individuals and groups do not have their own views on what is considered sexy.

ourselves being 'turned on' by either of these age groups. Whatever floats your boat, they say, but I feel there are some worrying implications here; men who pressure their girlfriends to do the Triple X being just one. (Of course in saying this I recognise that women have the right to their own personal choices.)

Then there is the eyebrow removal. Let's just put a pencil line there instead. But we are not clowns! Our faces are our faces; this is not a play and no one's filming. So why all the face paint? Can anyone else see the insanity of all this? *We are becoming less real.* And why? Because television, advertising and medical technology conveniently supports the current stereotype of what a human being should look like. Yet all its creating is women who can't cry, or not smile, because of all the botox, and women who constantly feel bad about themselves. It's ironic that men seem not to suffer so much with the beauty maintenance and plastic surgery, though I know many get work done (particularly the Hollywood actors). But the focus on women as the prime sex objects of society is reaching epidemic proportions.

As a woman who has had a breast lump removed, I find it extremely difficult to understand why a woman would get her breast cut open purely for reasons of vanity.

Yes, I understand that some plastic surgery can have incredible benefits. Like to people who have had accidents or need facial reconstruction. And for women with breasts so large it impedes their everyday living or for those that need breast reconstruction. Plastic surgery, in these cases, is obviously warranted and it is great that those in need can benefit from the medical technology. But they are not the people who concern me. It is rather all the men and women who change their bodies to conform to society's image of 'good-looking'. It is all the women who religiously remove the hair from their bodies; who collectively spend billions of dollars on the make-up market; who spend as much on clothes, hair accessories and jewellery; who live each moment concerned about their physical appearance. What a way to spend a lifetime.

And even after all this spending—enough to feed billions, or even solve the energy crisis—would you believe? All those women are just as worried about their appearance as they were to begin with. Nothing's changed! It's an endless cycle. And they will never 'get there', to a place where they feel beautiful enough, because they can't do that without maintenance. Hair grows back, make-up fades, people age. Of course many women may enjoy 'looking good' without being excessively beauty conscious, but you'll be hard-pressed to find one that says she feels pretty without wearing make-up.

I hope you understand that the image of 'thin' and 'good-looking' in society's current projection (in the 1800s it was curves, now it's bones) is a look limited to a minority of the people that make up that society. So all those billions of dollars to that endless array of marketing and advertising companies only do any good for a small portion of society. 'Looks' according to 'them' (society's projected image) is only *one* idea of beauty. But, beauty is in the eye of the beholder! What is beautiful to you; is. What is beautiful to me; is. But due to constant brainwashing many people are convinced that there is only one beautiful and that is the image they all compare themselves against. I'm telling you, it's a set-up, and we are all the victims. Those of us that stay true to ourselves know what we believe to be visually beautiful. Those of us who go deeper know that beauty cannot be measured by what we look like; beauty *is* life itself.

And if you consider yourself to be outside of society's image of beauty, you gotta know that you are being brainwashed by 'Big Brother'—the corporate machine. 'Keep them busy', the eerie voice says. 'Yes, let's just label as beautiful only a handful of people, and then the rest will pay, pay, pay.' And it's not just money they pay. It's a lifetime of guilt and self-torture that they 'just don't look like that'.

Please do not choose this for your life. Please understand that all human beings are beautiful because of who they are, it has absolutely nothing to do with how they look. If you begin any self-healing, or healing of others, know that you will begin to radiate a light and a love more beautiful and stunning than the most famous Hollywood actors. Being real is beautiful. Being plastic is just fake. Healing is our only salvation. I love you for who and what you are! For the light that resonates in you! For the love that you could share with our planet and its people! Just remember that *being yourself* will bring you love, real love. Real love will love how you look no matter how you look. And learning to love yourself for who you *really are,* and who you *really can be,* will give you a deep inner satisfaction, humming happily along with your re-awakened humanity.

Ideas and Solutions:

- Whatever your issue, I strongly recommend meditation, Yoga, Tai Chi. You need to help your body feel wonderful, once you stop hating and despising it, you will give it a chance to regain health by making it *feel good!* Very important.
- Note your facial expressions. Do you try to look a certain way to people? If so, a lot of your time may be spent thinking about how others view you. Try to go beyond that, actually *be*ing with people, with a neutral face and relaxed demeanour.
- Please watch *Super Size Me*.[99] Allow yourself to get angry at the fast food corporations who are recklessly endangering our health without any moral or ethical considerations.
- Put all the money you put into beauty into humanity or your life's dream.
- Remember, my fellow women sisters: If we all did this (let the hair grow back, give up the make-up etc.) we would be rebelling together! We are protected in numbers. The masses accept what the masses do. We could turn this whole world around if we starved the beauty industry of finance and put that money into politics or social change. To achieve this goal all that is needed is to start a fashion trend (it would help if some celebs got on board) whereby it's 'cool' to be natural; i.e., no make-up or shaving etc. Just think of the savings. Yes, many women say,

---

[99] A documentary of one man attempting to eat nothing but Macca's (McDonalds) for 30 days.

'I do it because it makes me feel good'; I just wonder if they would say the same thing if it was considered unpopular in society to wear make-up or shave.

- An excellent relaxation technique is to mentally tell parts of your body to relax. One name for this technique is called Auto-suggestion; this example is used during the final relaxation pose of a Yoga session. (Of course you can do it anytime you want.) "I relax the toes, I relax the toes. The toes *are* relaxed. I relax the calves, I relax the calves. The calves *are* relaxed."[100] Repeat for all areas of the body. It can help to physically tense and release each area before saying or thinking the above instructions.

---

[100] Lidell, p. 27.

Chapter 10 – Self-criticism

"One must put oneself in every one's position. To understand everything is to forgive everything."[101]

As a prelude to the next chapter, I would like to share my true beliefs about the nature of self-criticism. I believe many of us suffer from it, including me. But what are the main things we criticise ourselves about? Aside from anything and everything it is often when we're struggling to cope that we are hardest on ourselves. It's ironic that the time we need our own strength the most can be the time we become our own worst enemy. We look at 'Society' (not them again!) and we see families, workers, and people taking holidays and driving around in cars and shopping and we think, 'Wow, they're normal, what the hell's wrong with me?'. We assume that everyone else is coping when, in fact, many people are suffering exactly the way you may be right now. Our lives are individual and unique, but our problems; physical, mental and emotional, are shared by others—however many, there are people out there who could relate. We need to realise that we are pretty good at being self-destructive. We can destroy ourselves mentally and one way we do it is through self-criticism.

Just say I was having a bad time and got upset or angry and then started railing at myself about what I'd done, or what I didn't do, and what an idiot I was, etc. Then when this state doesn't help me at all, I'm even more confused, upset and angry. Then I may think, 'Now all

---

[101] L Tolstoy, *War and Peace,* Pan Books Ltd, London, 1972. First published 1904, p. 108.

I've done is hurt myself and I still have the original problem'. Then the self-criticism may turn into, 'What the hell's wrong with me? How did it get this far? Why can't I be "normal" and cope?' The answer for me at this point is to truly analyse and learn the root cause of why I am upset; to get to the core of what really is bothering me. But the thing is, is that I could do that entire process without any self-criticism. "To understand everything is to forgive everything."[102] Because once you understand the nature of the problem, it is much easier to develop compassion. Whatever 'fuck up' happens, we can *always* turn to healing. We can learn from every situation, rather than regret any situation. To grow, we need to change by learning more. Self-criticism is not going to help us to become better people, only the healing of self-criticism could.

Self-criticism literally eats away at the self. It doesn't accept or understand the natural problems that life poses and the natural human reactions. If you suffer in this way at all I ask you: *Would you ever say those words or express those thoughts to a child or to any other human being?* If you wouldn't, what makes you any different from others? You are a human being too!

A great hypocrisy occurs when we refuse to take care of ourselves mentally, emotionally and spiritually and then subsequently find constant examples in our external world of people not caring about us. If you do not eat when you're hungry, you won't feel 'full' and this colours the way you feel about yourself and about others. When you feel 'crap' you may blame the world around you for it, when it is possible that to feel better

---

[102] Tolstoy, p. 108.

all you need to do is drink some water, eat healthily, and practise relaxation. If you're drinking yourself into a stupor it would be easy to feel uncared for because you may have already become withdrawn and stopped letting other people in. If you're hurting yourself it's a lot easier to feel hurt by others because you're already hurting. You may think that others don't care but *you* must care about *yourself.*

One of the worst ways we hurt ourselves is with our thoughts. When we do this we are not loving and accepting our brain and emotions. We are ultimately criticising our own right to exist, as we are right now, and this fundamental flaw makes us miserable.

Yes, we have many complex issues to deal with. But we can deal with them all through accepting that all humans suffer from these dilemmas in one way or another. Accepting, without self-destructing, is the key. "To understand everything is to forgive everything."[103] We need to forgive ourselves for being self-critical in order to heal the condition.

---

[103] Tolstoy, p. 108.

Chapter 11 – Self-abuse

"Can't you see the people that have been abused, they figure out a way they can take control, they just learn to destroy themselves"[104]

Right here, right now, I want to apologise if my words have upset anybody. This is not my intention. Just know that I endeavour to make clear what I can. I am not saying that life is easy, because I know that many people are very unhappy in countries throughout even the Free World right now, and I want to address these people personally.

I am sorry.

I am sorry for everyone that has hurt you. I am sorry for all the ways you have hurt yourself. I have always felt this empathy for others, because I know we all suffer, even though our own suffering seems so personal. Our empathy must also include ourselves. So I am sorry for all the ways I have hurt myself. We are only human, and we must learn together that there are better ways of handling our pain than taking it out on ourselves or others. The hardest thing for any child/person to come to terms with is the fact that they have been abused by their own parents or care-givers. It is very hard for this growing person to understand that this is not right! For who would bring one into this world just to cause them suffering? Can you imagine the difficulty in a person whose own parents/carers have abused them to forgive? Yet I ask all those in this position to seek healing and

---

[104] Jess Hieser, *Meaning of life,* unreleased music single, Jess Hieser, 2007.

forgiveness, not for their abusers sake but for their own.

We are each a unique divine expression of life and it is our duty to become who we are.

If one has been abused, one is never who abused them; one is the evidence of hurt and of pain, and this pain is felt because one desires love and peace! All who have ever felt hurt only wanted to be loved. Therefore all must love, rather than hurt. One must demonstrate compassion regardless of what others do. I understand how some of you may think, 'It's all well and good to say that, but what can I do? Who's helping me?' And I must make this clear:

The only person we can ever truly help is ourselves.

No matter how much love and healing we spread throughout the world, it is the people we help that must take responsibility for their own healing. In truth many need to first help themselves by being open to receiving. But if you rescued a starving child you would still need to help him learn to develop his own self-esteem and sense of security, before he could look after himself just as well. If you take a woman who has suffered abuse and put her in a loving relationship, she will still have to learn to take care of herself before she could accept true love, otherwise she may project any hurt feelings onto the new partner no matter how loving they are. You can lead a horse to water but you can't make it drink. You get the idea. What do we do when we truly support somebody? We act as a guide if they need assistance. We direct them towards themselves and their own truths. We remind them that the strength is within *them*. Think of how we may act with a friend, if he/she

124

wanders off the track, we gently guide their arm back to the road (or remind them that they are already on the road!), so that they can continue to walk the path on their own.

We must accept that everything we have experienced makes us who we are today. Rather than fight against it, we must learn to understand it, and then use that understanding to help us overcome life's obstacles, and learn life's lessons. It seems some lessons need to be learnt many times before we actually get them, enough to change, and then move on. But through each lesson we expand as people, taking in more knowledge, more understanding, until the realisation dawns on us that being consciously aware of who we are is actually how we grow.

The only person we can ever truly heal is ourselves.

It is solely our responsibility to heal ourselves. This does not mean we cannot have help! Far from it! Reach out as far and wide as you can for assistance. Just know that you will do the bulk of it, simply because you know yourself better than anyone. It takes inner work to heal. To heal, plainly means, to feel whole. To be content with everything *you* are, regardless of the situation. Sometimes, it may simply take a change in attitude. If you are in a terrible situation, your only choice is to survive. Survive until you can escape the situation, which I pray you can. In some situations, people may feel trapped, when they are not physically trapped. There may be mental conditioning that needs to be recognised before one can choose to release it. Some may make more fatal choices which I cannot judge, I can only pray and send compassion to those of you who are here, and hope you can find peace in this lifetime. I pray that there is a way for you to heal; can you see what you would need to do to make that happen?

I can promise you, that if you can learn to accept your true self with compassion, you will choose a life that is rewarding and wonderful in every way.

Now. When we are children, we have little control over our external environment. Some children choose to work on relationships almost immediately, by asking their parents from very young ages, 'What's wrong?' or 'Why are you mad at me?' Children trying to gauge their parents' emotions so they can find out where on earth they stand. Unfortunately if the parents aren't communicative, or only communicate negative, fixed-minded attitudes and emotions, then it is totally left up to the child to figure out what the hell is going on, and why their family or parent(s) seem unhappy and also treat them very badly.

A child who has been abused in any way is very likely going to learn to hate or punish themselves in some way and often in similar ways to their abusive upbringing. (For example, those who were brought up in a fearful environment, as adults may become overly cautious; still ruled by fear in their own minds. Some may also emulate their parent's bad habits, addictions or behaviours, which, even if they don't realise it, helps them form an understanding, and even compassion for how their parents behaved or may have suffered.) It is very hard for this growing person to understand the psychology of self-hatred, to know that they need and deserve lots of love and care, and a life where they can still fulfil their dreams. Maybe they never had any

126

dreams, only anger. And until they can give up that anger, they will never be able to see or realise the dream. The hardest fact for those who have experienced personal suffering is that no matter how good others are to them, they may never see these opportunities if they are still dealing with unresolved misery. If they are judging others deeply for their actions, they are probably judging themselves similarly. If they truly believe there is no hope, the only way they will find any solace is to take all necessary channels to find inner peace.

I cannot speak for those who have suffered great tragedies. I can only say that I am so incredibly sorry that you have had to suffer this, it pains and tears at my heart the enormity of your grief, but I believe if there was enough love in this world, you may feel a little better, and may even be able to help alleviate others' suffering, and perhaps, in time, allow others to alleviate yours.

One to the practice of things we let go, and
One to the tears of the things we let go of, and
One to the moment we live in right now, and
One to the East West North and South[105]

I have so much love for all of you in the world. For all those beautiful people who have and haven't suffered. For all those who understand (and don't understand) that everyone deserves love, it is a human right, synonymous with the human heart. We are not given hearts so that they would be empty of love. We have hearts to feel and know the joys of being filled with

---

[105] Michael Franti & Spearhead, *East to the West,* 2006.

love.

If you can learn to love your *self,* by honouring your self in all situations, you open up your heart to receive others' love in ways you never imagined. Love resonates to love, the more you have the more you have the more you have. But it must come from you first.

I am saying what I know to be the truth. If you have been traumatised in the past and want to heal, you must forgive yourself if needed and let go of the pain others have caused. You need to accept that No One deserves to be treated badly. You couldn't choose where you lived as a child. You can only strive to get strong and become an adult and then try to gain control over your own existence. The hurt child inside you still needs to feel love and support and live in a safe environment, just as you do.

> The adults around you when you were a child may not have known how to comfort you at that time. Now *you* are the adult in your life, and if you're not comforting the child within you, then that is very sad indeed. What was done in the past is done, and it is over now. But this is present time, and you now have the opportunity to treat yourself the way you wish to be treated … *Begin to love and approve of yourself.* That's what that little child needs in order to express itself at its highest potential.[106]

Help is there for the asking. Being afraid of help is like being afraid of the guy who's lifting you out of the rattlesnake cage. Holding onto pride only makes people more miserable. I have never felt there was anything

---

[106] Hay, p. 61.

wrong with asking for help. Quite the opposite. When you allow someone to truly help you, they have just raised the level of your existence, which in turn raises the level of their existence. It feels good to help others; therefore it feels good to receive from others. Don't even question it. Show appreciation, yes! Don't use people, yes! But accept that if you need help, there is probably someone out there whose life it would enrich to offer it.

If you've always wanted something but never gone for it, go for it! Honour yourself and you are honouring your own highest good.

Don't let fear hold you back! You only live once!

Yes! In our current consciousness this is the one lifetime we have! *This* is the time to live our dreams. Once we sort ourselves out we can make an extraordinary impact on the world. At the very least, in doing what we love, we are neutral and self-content. We can learn to be healers; we are all born healers and it's just a matter of reviving the memory. We are born healers because we need each others love to survive. Why do we all inherently believe that children should be loved? Many studies show that children raised without love and affection are adversely affected. Children grow into adults; we are all human beings. It is love that truly enriches our existence; that gives us a sense of purpose. We all deserve more love than our hearts can yet imagine. It's all there, *so what are we going to do?* "Is love enough ... or can you love some more?"[107] We need a world full of conscious healers, to

---

[107] Michael Franti & Spearhead, *Can you love some more?,*

129

heal ourselves, and all those around us (globally), and then to heal the earth itself or perhaps all three simultaneously.

> And it's not just me, it's everyone, afraid of who they could become thinking the outside world is never gonna change, but it just takes one, to get things done, adds to the total sum of the people willing to fight for a saner world
> So will you get up? Join with us, the peaceful and the just; all it takes is to nurture your own heart[108]

Ideas and Solutions:

- Please trust that once you can open up to someone, once you believe that there is hope, that the will of the human spirit is mighty and can take you wherever you want to go. Believe that others can help, and they can. Just remember each human being is walking around in their own headspace, trying to overcome their own issues, whatever they may be. Be willing to see others, and to allow others to see you. Be open to healing, be open to changing; and I send love to all those suffering.

- I do believe Louise L Hay's book *You can heal your life* is an excellent do-it-yourself healing manual. If you can overcome any judgments you may have and be willing to use the tools with an open heart, its possible; you really can heal your life. Sounds corny I know, but that's a

---

2006.
[108] Jess Hieser, *Meaning of life,* unreleased music single, Jess Hieser, 2007.

judgment. It is not necessarily healthy that many of us are cynical about the processes, avenues and even the terms of healing, whatever they are. We must release these outmoded judgments if we are to allow ourselves to accept healing, (much needed by all humans), in any of its shapes or forms.

- If you are hurting yourself or living in a negative way, sometimes simply adding some good into your life can put you on the road to recovery. For instance, rather than a smoker or alcoholic trying to quit, they could commit to a daily walk and drinking more water. For negative thinking, one could choose to annul one self-criticism a day with a single thought 'I love and accept myself'. Sometimes adding good into a dark situation is the best way to gradually come out of it.

- One of the ultimate healing techniques is to wish no harm, and even to send love to those that have hurt you. I know some people may think this is insane, but it is one way that may help restore our power, by maintaining human decency, regardless of others' actions. I have come to appreciate those experiences that I once perceived as terrible, because everything I have experienced has made me who I am today, and I need to accept all that I am to be at peace.

Chapter 12 – Choosing power over peace

Is it only me, or could the world live in peace? Is it only me, or do *all* humans have the capacity for good and just need it to be nurtured? Is it only me, or is it true that if *all* children were brought up in a loving environment that we could have a world built on love and peace? Is it only me who believes that World Peace is actually possible? I know within me that my heart is filled with love, that I wish nothing more for the world than an end to all human, animal and earth suffering, that I believe if current and future fascists could be re-educated from birth or even now that they could become peace makers, that we can all learn to love and heal ourselves and each other, that the only reason such terrible things, such as torture, ever occur is because people are brainwashed from a very young age and learn to fear, hate and despise an enemy, one that is often created from their own country's actions.

America fears losing control, so it goes to extreme lengths to have *all* the control, all the time. It (the empire) does not understand the meaning of 'share'. Indeed, it would see sharing as a giving away of its power, only appropriate when it's in their own interest to do so. The U.S. empire believes if it lets go of the reins for even a second, all its power will be taken over by the next most powerful country.

Everything they do is driven by the fear that they will lose their current position of power.

But how many souls are sold to the devil to keep it? I mean, they have to control *whole countries* to achieve this. They have to have a rope around the world that

132

says, 'We are the only ones with the power to pull this noose tighter'. They have to have average beings tortured and shattered in the name of the war against terrorism. They need scapegoats, say take anyone from the Middle East, or who *looks like* they're from the Middle East. They are openly displaying their hatred towards the Muslim world. But the noose is around their necks too. Like every dictatorship, once the government becomes too radical or extremist, it may be overthrown and replaced by what seems to be a moderate government, which may then turn into another fascist regime. If we could just topple these current radical governments, wouldn't it be nice to put some Reiki masters at the helm, along with some academics, artists, scholars, and philosophers; turn the whole world in another direction, one where people are able to use their own resources to support themselves, without having those resources allocated to the greedy men in power?

If my yearly wage could feed some of the poor in this world, I would happily trade that in and go live in the bush growing my own veggies. I believe we underestimate how much we would be willing to forego if it meant millions of our fellow humans could end the poverty and misery in their lives.

How much would you give up of your life of luxury now, so that mass starvation could be stemmed and vaccines brought to where they are needed? We could be doing so much right now if the people in this country were willing.

Ah, yes, the sceptics. Ok, so when the governments of those countries we donate to themselves are corrupt, very little of the foreign aid may get through. It may turn into Mercedes-Benz's and government palaces. The best way to get money into poverty stricken countries is to know people who will pass it on directly. But c'mon, how close do you think the 1st World leaders are with these countries? Who makes billions of dollars off Blacks and Easterners working for less than a dollar a day? We do!! That's right, it's the 1st World that is taking all the profits out of those countries and putting them into our own pockets. Why pay workers here $20 an hour when you could pay the Indonesians 20¢ an hour? I believe the wage for a call centre job here is 40 thousand odd dollars a year. So most companies outsource; in India the wage for the same job is only a few thousand dollars a year. 3 mobile is but one example of this. Humanity is not in the hearts of any 1st World country, only money is. Only money and power and more money and more power.

These countries do not care that millions and millions of people have died and will die from diseases that we, the 1st World, have vaccines to prevent and medicines to cure. They starve while we eat our fancy food in our fancy restaurants. We get our goods Made in China, exploiting foreign workers there and everywhere for our own 'prosperity'. We are starving those millions of people with our own greed.

And this is what really sickens me. The people in power not only know this, they endorse it. They are starved of hearts and souls. They are buddy-buddy in private with those governments that commit atrocities. The U.S. say they 'care about Darfur' knowing China will veto every humanitarian bill they seek to pass. (Basically there's a lot of mining resources in Sudan, which China does very well from, ignoring human rights abuses there.)

134

But the militia in Sudan was known to boil and eat babies for Christ's sake. Women are being raped and people are being tortured under many brutal regimes. 4 million killed in the Congo in less than a decade! But where is America? Why aren't they feeding Africa, or destroying the Junjaweed militia and the Sudanese government? Why are they spending *trillions of dollars on a war* when they could eliminate every preventable disease and feed everyone? And not one single human would have to suffer the penalty of being born into a 3rd World country. I hope you can see that if America has all this power and they wanted World Peace, they could help to create it. I hope you can see that they have (or had) the wealth to eliminate poverty and even conflict, the world over.

Some important points need to be made here for those who may still question, or not understand the reality of how the West suppresses liberty and opportunity for those who have very little power to fight for their rights. Aside from the horrific nature of violence and war in many poor countries, there is also the disgraceful policies of international agencies such as the International Monetary Fund (IMF) and the World Bank, which set agricultural subsidies for the sale of produce which only benefits the rich countries, leaving the poorer countries near starvation as they cannot sell their products at the competitive rates, let alone pay the high sale taxes. Also, the reason diseases in the 3rd World aren't being cured or prevented is because pharmaceutical companies are only given financial endorsement for making products which they can sell; and they sell in 1st World countries! There is no profit made in giving the poor what they need, so they continue to die every day. Of course with the obscene profits that pharmaceutical companies make they could afford to vaccinate Africa, and cure many diseases, without going bankrupt themselves. Obviously if governments and rich citizens were taxed a small amount, this would cover costs too. This is why the world is truly nuts. Only an inclusive World government implementing fair and equitable global laws, incorporating a more democratic and accountable UN, International Criminal Court and World parliament would be able to tackle these issues. World public opinion is also extremely important in the fight to overturn these barbaric practices. Wouldn't this be a much better way to create real democracy? Yet in America's case it is their foreign policy agenda that is one of the key factors in preventing it (as they have substantial weight in agencies such as the IMF and World Bank). Their history of resource reaping in the world is prolific, along with the neglect of their own citizens.

I believe that we are capable of so much more than we think. If humans can create so much bad, imagine how much good they could create? Some humans seem to have been 'set to evil'; you can pick them out of the crowd because they will always be telling you how evil the people they're oppressing are. They will bomb in the name of being bombed. An eye for an eye for an eye for an eye … Doesn't anybody know there is no end to that cycle?

We don't even know yet the capacity of the human brain, let alone the human heart. If we are capable of so much evil, it makes sense that we are capable of so much good. The Universe has to balance, right? Well, I tell you what, if we balanced out the human history of evil, we could have peace for a long, long time.

I know this and I believe this with all my heart and soul.

If I am capable of all this passion, what are you capable of? How much passion do you feel for yourself and the world? If we understand the true humanity that lives within our very being, we connect with one of the most powerful and unlimited energies on earth. Many powers have we forgotten; now is the time to remember. Much yet for us to discover; now is the time to learn. Great changes are occurring with every move we make. Even if we cannot achieve peace in this world, and in this lifetime, we can certainly leave an indelible mark that is absolutely necessary for the survival and well-being of future generations.

Chapter 13 – Violent computer games

Let me paint you a picture: Human figures are shot through the chest; the legs; the head. Blood spurts everywhere. More figures are shot. The bodies lay wounded or dead on the ground. There's blood all over the walls. A variety of weapons are used, designed to cause fatality.

Am I describing reality, like that which occurs in war, or does this also accurately describe what I call a 'death game'?

Granted, some of the death games involve killing aliens or creatures that 'aren't quite human'. But then why is the colour of blood in most games always red? And why do the creatures seem so 'human-like'?

One of the main differences between real war and the war-like games is that in the games they always count the dead. That's the whole point.

Think of the same picture again. Simultaneously, while real humans are killing real humans, with all the horrors involved, young men and boys play death games for hours on end, against each other on the net, on their PC, using real named weapons, with the same simulated capacity as weapons of war. They are glued to their screens and can become addicted to the game, but do they know that if they joined the Army, they could be doing this for real?

How can the simulation of killing not be detrimental to a young man or woman's humanity?

The whole counter argument of, 'But it's only a game, it's not real'; how does this justify the use of games that simulate mass killing with weapons that exist in the real world for any reason? It is just a farther indoctrination of the 'good guys/bad guys' concept. It doesn't matter how many or how brutally the bad guys (game enemies) are killed as long as it's the good guys (game players) doing the killing. Do you know that the makers of *America's Army* take footage to use in their game *straight off the front lines in Iraq?* This is an Army training game, which is also accessible to the masses! And if I was a person in Iraq who had been injured in this war, seen real death and destruction, lost my loved ones, with no country coming to my aid, with other countries *destroying* me, and I knew that the boys and men of the world (and possibly girls and women) were sitting on their arses simulating the actions of my downfall, having fun with it ... I can tell you it makes me sick to my very soul.

Who are the ones that fight in the armies and wars? Men, mainly. Who are the ones who play the war games? Men, mainly. These young men[109] of the world who play these games, imagine if they all fought for humanity? Do you know how much power is in these young minds to do good in the world? This is why it's so important for those in power to control them, by saturating them with violence; as the potential of young men and all men in these democratic countries is huge. Although women are gaining more equality on some

---

[109] Although I know these games are becoming more popular with women—which I find frightening—it is still predominantly men who are supporting the violent game industry, hence the male references from here on in.

levels, it is still generally easier for a man to rise through the ranks of any profession, to make a decent wage, to become professors, scientists, writers, intellects. It is still a 'man's world', i.e. mainly ruled by men. It is men, mostly, who are the millionaires and heads of corporations. Imagine if they used their money to support changes in government that would make society more humane for all of us. Imagine if all the men who play these war games, chose to fight for peace.

But any males I meet who play these games, in response to my views that they may breach their humanity, very proudly and defiantly say that they stick by their 'right' to play them. They respond to my views by saying: 'It's only a game'.

Only a game. What does that really mean? It's just like with violence on TV, except you're interacting. I have spoken previously of my thoughts on the damage caused by violence on television. We have seen so many thousands (possibly millions) of gunshots, stabbings, fights, blood, dead bodies, *simulated* on television. None of it is 'real', yet we are still experiencing the watching of this simulated bloodshed and violence, and that is real!

Just like with TV, if you are playing these games, the images are directly imprinted into your brain and into your memory. Where do these images go? And what happens when you watch real violence on a screen? Where do these images go? Is it possible that the brain doesn't know the difference between the simulated and the real images?

Is it possible that the makers and the sellers of the

violent games and movies know this? And that none of it is blocked by governments because they know this?

Is it possible that some can no longer distinguish between real violence, footage of war, etc., and that which they see on their TV and in their death games? (Of course people may well be able to but I still encourage deep thought on these matters.)

Perhaps like with the Hollywood films, they get the, 'I achieved something' feelings. The ones they need to propel them towards their life's dream.

Like television and other multi-media, we can become addicted to the pull of 'the machine'. Similar to in the *Matrix* film, we 'plug in' every time we watch TV or play any computer game. (Just think of what it looks like from the hypothetical aliens' point of view.) When playing games, one may feel a devilish urge to 'finish the task'. I call it devilish because sometimes we feel we must keep playing even against our will. I have found this in myself, becoming momentarily addicted to playing *Tetris* on my mobile phone. Ridiculous I know, but there is something in the mind that likes the colours and the lights, and the escapism (the feeling that time ceases to exist because we become so engrossed) of computer games, and if we can't beat our own high score, we may feel we have to keep playing until we do. It is a part of human nature to want to solve problems, to finish what we start, so games utilise this trait perfectly in terms of creating addiction. Have you heard the stories of people who have died after playing games for days on end? This demonstrates how addictive computer games can be. But I ask you to consider the difference in the influence from addiction to a game like

141

Tetris compared to a game like *Quake*. Addiction to the machines is nasty enough, let alone addiction to machines spewing brutal gore.

It *does* matter what we choose to fill our heads with—of course it does! If we studied history or art or philosophy; read the great novelists; listened to the great musicians of any and all cultures etc., we are hearing the sounds, and reading the words of others who have thirsted to gain mastery of their craft; a valuable human pursuit. This can inform and inspire us in our own pursuits. All this technology is satisfying only a very small part of us. We need self-reflection, insightful conversations, mind explorations, and *love* to truly eke out the passion and beauty of this existence. The longer we have the suppress button on, the more we slaughter our senses, the closer we come to forgetting what sensibilities are. We will, and we are, in fact, de-humanising.

I am interested in how many players of these games feels pain or anger or *any*thing when they watch real violence on TV or the Internet.

How many of them vote Liberal?

I was on a train one day going to Box Hill when a bunch of private school boys from an elite college boarded. I couldn't help but hear their conversation about a death game they all played. They were explicitly describing different uses of weapons, how many kills they had clocked up (frags, they call them), laughing and jesting with each other about what they would do, or had done, and so on. To give you an example: 'Did you see when I blew Franga's arm off with the rocket launcher? Fucken awesome'.

My back was turned to them. I was reading an article in *The Age,* World section, about some recent bloodshed in Iraq. The boys actually referred to a weapon that was mentioned in this particular article. I was looking at a picture of a child who had lost limbs. To hear them laughing and joking about killing, blowing arms off etc., and with real named weapons, was both surreal and horrifying. I couldn't help but request that they cease talking in this way and explained to them that what they were describing was very similar to what I was reading in *The Age* about an incident in Iraq. They took it quite well and ceased talking about their 'game'. The very next line I heard was: 'Mum didn't make me the sandwich I wanted today'.

It's safe to say that many 'well-off' boys are playing these games (of course many who are poor would play too, but it isn't cheap to buy high-tech computers with top notch graphics, let alone the games themselves, though many know how to burn or trade necessary items). To me it seems many of these boys are detached from what is happening in the real world. Yet more recently I have met some young men who play death games that are reasonably in tune with world affairs and seemingly quite left-wing. But in talking with them about my ideas they still couldn't make the connection. They view the games as fantasy and are unwilling to acknowledge that many of them are steeped in reality. Nor could they accept the truth that simulated killing cannot be healthy. Perhaps it can be an outlet for anger, but there are healthier ways to express this, such as writing down all your thoughts, having a good cry, being honest with the object of your anger, etc. To go 'bang bang' for hours on a computer game may or may not be helpful to anger management, but, unlike the other healthier options I've listed here, it is possible that playing death games may even exacerbate or incite anger in some people.

My personal belief is that all this violence in games and on TV is *designed* to desensitise these young men to *all* violence; they are encouraged to feel that it is cool without any moral ramifications. First-shooter games are a prime example of this; eliciting feelings of power and pride in the player, about their knowledge of weapon usage, combat strategies, ways of maiming etc. And what happens to men who are proud about their power as men to wield violence and have control over violence? Aren't they the kind of men who run the world?

By instilling this pride for violence in our young men, corporations (with government consent) are appealing to that very inner nature, that same inner nature that is destroying people the world over.

In light of all this, tell me again that it is *just a game*.

A game about war is not what I'd call a game. I'd call it a modified simulation of the same thing. War.

A game of simulated mass slaughter with simulated blood all over the walls; blood players create with their simulated gunshots, is not what I'd call a game. I'd call it a copy, a version, of real life horror.

Can you imagine the young boy in the war torn country, picking up his first gun at five, seeing people around him die, learning how to hate the enemy, and become a soldier, so that killing becomes his way of life?

Can you imagine the boy in the free democratic country, picking up his first toy gun at five, over time learning to play violent games, and watching violence on TV, seeing simulations of many people die, until he grows up to love playing being the soldier, being the gunman on his computer games, and simulated killing plays a strong role in his life? There are many children under ten who play their older sibling's games; with parents who either don't know or don't care.

I find the parallels very ominous and very telling.

Society isn't just like this because that's how things worked out. It is ultimately controlled by governments and laws, what you can and can't do and the social acceptance of those laws; the general consensus. How much money you can make, how many laws you can break and get away with breaking. The highest of the lawbreakers are the lawmakers.

Governments ban material they see unfit for the general populace. But the game *Grand Theft Auto* isn't one of them (anymore). I understand the problem of banning, that it makes the game even more desirable, and I agree that this is not the solution. It goes a lot deeper than that. We need to question and understand why such material is created in the first place. What devious reasons lay behind it? And why do we, as a society, accept it? *Any game about killing is a complete insult to all those who are being killed in our world!!* Men who make fortunes from the violent game industry are only helping the government's agenda, in more ways than one. The violent game industry is worth *billions*. Governments collect tax—from many industries—and then start allocating money to their war funds.

It is all interconnected. We are surrounded by simulated violence for a reason! We have it slammed down our throats, especially men. A young man would be made to feel a 'pussy' if he wasn't interested in violence in some way. He should either fight or be tough in the real world or like fighting and being tough in the game world. If a boy of 15 didn't want to watch *Die Hard 4.0* his peers may even start questioning his sexuality. It's outrageous! But the fact is if the majority of men gave up their addiction to simulated violence, corporations and industries would lose billions. Yet addiction is a powerful thing and I wonder how many could understand the validity of giving up those addictions? Yet that would be true power; rendering billionaires bankrupt.

I am not saying that all of the above is true for all men. There are many intelligent young men, striving for a greater understanding of themselves and of life. But they're not the ones I am worried about.

And as for the indoctrinated boys, you know what? It is not their fault. The way society is set up, they just can't avoid it. They lean towards the majority, because most people feel *safer* leaning towards the majority. Not standing out. And the way things are it is just drummed in over and over again. Simulated violence is fine; even real violence is fine and often applauded. (Not to mention the huge increase in animated female characters with disproportionately large breasts; indoctrinating men's view of sexuality, and the blurred lines of using female combat characters; endorsing simulated violence against women.) All the while the corporate advertising screams, *'You want this!!'* Exactly like with TV, they sell it to you in such a way as to make you believe that you already want it. The TV/game says, 'You requested the violence, this is what you like'. And you completely forgot that *you never asked for it!* It's just what was already there. The majority of people conform to what the majority of people believe is acceptable. This is the society we have become.

Imagine if a percentage of sales for every violent game sold, was donated to Red Cross.

Imagine if the young men of the world weren't swamped in simulated violence, and proud of it.

What sort of men would these become?

Ideas and Solutions:

- If you want to do a quick check on how much influence computer games are having in your life, draw a chart of your activities and the time spent on them. You could span this over a week or five years, (just do rough estimates). For instance, how many frags have you clocked up over how much time? How much time spent watching TV? How much time spent walking, relaxing, reading, writing, reflecting, following your life's dream, etc.? Once you've done a rough chart look at how high the levels are for violent games or TV and measure against the time taken for personal growth.

- Some players say that playing violent games increases their confidence, plus they get to 'meet' people online and learn about role playing, decision making and different game techniques. I still say that good old fashioned social interaction and learning that which will be practised in the *real* world, are far healthier and more productive pursuits than that which can be gained via simulation.

- *Good Game* is amongst a new breed of TV shows that review games, including ones graphically violent. Using terms like 'war' and 'grenade' in game review is normal, when this in fact completely disrespects all those at war right now! Please Wake Up World!!

- Consider that the first-shooter game *Call of Duty 4: Modern Warfare,* has sold over 13 million copies since 2007.[110] This figure is close to the current amount of displaced refugees from Iraq, Palestine and Afghanistan combined from recent conflicts (over 15 million). On the one hand, you have the players of *Call of Duty 4: Modern Warfare,* and on the other you have real people who have fled from war. Is this not a frightening circumstance? What would happen if both these groups could be swapped for a day? Do you think those refugees would want to play a realistic war game? If you think they wouldn't, and consider why they wouldn't, ask yourself why it is that you do.

---

[110] http://en.wikipedia.org/wiki/Call_of_Duty_4_Modern_ Warfare
Sales at May 2009. Accessed on July 19th 2009.

Chapter 14 – Addictions in society

"Everyone addicted to the same nicotine
Everyone addicted to the same gasoline
Everyone addicted to a technicolor screen
Everybody tryin' get their hands on the same green"[111]

When the word addiction is mentioned people tend to think of addiction to cigarettes, or drugs, or computer games (!), but what about addiction to certain emotional states? Without realising it, we can become addicted to the emotional rush that occurs in certain situations, when the chemicals we read as 'feelings' are released from the brain. Basically, we get used to our own reactions to external situations which may then become a pattern that we find hard to break, especially if we are continually walking down the same mental pathways; we can only break them by changing our own response.[112] For instance, if we know we usually feel defensive when confronted by another, we can practise deep breathing when it happens, or a number of other strategies. But as it is with any addiction, if we fuel the habit/response, by repeating it often, the addiction grows. It's the same with anger. If you allow yourself to get angry in situations where it has gone beyond asserting your needs to demanding them, or when you feel you've acted badly, you may get angry at yourself for getting angry, and in so doing, possibly repeat the same situation that initially made you angry! Ok. So what to do? As mentioned last chapter, when anger or other aggressive emotions come on, go for a walk, take

---

[111] Michael Franti & Spearhead, *Yell Fire!,* 2006.
[112] For a thorough examination of this topic please see the documentary: *What the bleep do we know?*

some deep breaths, punch some pillows, scream into the open air, write down everything that's bothering you, and avoid people or situations that bring up the same emotion, or practise self-control in their presence. Look at the true root cause of your anger; what are you *really* angry about? The truth in these matters can often be enlightening. Once you find the cause perhaps you can deal with it better. It will at least give you a starting point from which you can begin to deal with the real problem, and consider possible changes you would need to make to resolve it. If you want to you can literally re-wire your own brain patterns, by consciously choosing to change your own reactions.

In talking of brain wiring, I am referring to the pathways that build in the brain according to what one thinks and does. Apparently it has been found that people who do cryptic crosswords have a reduced risk of developing Alzheimer's disease or suffering memory loss, because the lateral thinking needed to do cryptics connects one side of the brain to the other; more pathways are created, therefore a greater range of references can be accessed. This is an example of how the brain pathways work.

In relation to addictions we can build up certain pathways which may not be healthy. Just as we can eat unhealthily, we can think unhealthily too. I love these questions posed by Louise L Hay on this: "Would you really dig into yesterday's garbage to make tonight's meal? Do you dig into old *mental* garbage to create tomorrow's experiences?"[113] Negative thoughts can create strong pathways in the brain and if it becomes

---

[113] Hay, p. 26.

habitual to think like this we may not even realise how extensively negative that inner dialogue is; however, we can always start a new pathway anytime we want. Then it's important to be patient for the change as the new pathway is not yet well worn.

The 1st World in general seems addicted or 'used to' ignoring or avoiding important issues. The addiction to television and entertainment very much endorses this apathy because it takes up so much time outside of securing food and shelter. *The ability to fight for one's rights must always be present in human beings, not just when those rights are being violated, but most especially when there is inequality in the world, but one finds oneself in a good position.* Our apathy is actually killing our ability to love, to have compassion for all beings. This complacency is the reason we are not asking Howard to stand down for participating in war crimes.

Why aren't we using some of our time to make society better for all of us by talking with people about what could be done? Why are we so beset with our own needs and problems and greed, even as the world falls apart right before our very eyes? Isn't that important enough to talk about or get out of bed for? So why don't we? It is because we are addicted to our very lifestyle. In some ways we are even addicted to not caring. It's easier to put it in the 'too hard' basket.

We must recognise the debilitative nature of our addictions to negative emotions and mental states. If we choose to recognise it, we may see the connection between, 'every time we feel agitated we want a cigarette', or, 'every time we get angry we want a drink'. I believe it is our emotional addictions that give way to our physical addictions, so if we try to deal directly with the emotion involved, rather than focusing on the outer addiction, we may find it much easier to dissolve a physical addiction than we thought. My advice is to work out what you're addicted to and why. Work on dissolving all addictions through practising moderation. And don't ever give up hope in finding your own solutions.

And of course there is hope! Masses of people are awakening and will become human rights activists. They will be the local fruit shop owner, or the guy next door, they may not even know it yet, but it is happening to all of us. It is becoming very clear that how we live our own lives *does* have a radical effect on the world around us. Every time we choose not to drive a car, every time we recycle, every time we give help to someone who needs it, every time we think of how to create a more loving and peaceful world, we are creating a more loving and peaceful world. *There is hope, because if there is no hope there is failure.* And if we fail not only will human rights violations continue, but the planet itself may not be able to sustain us.

Ideas and Solutions:

- In relation to breaking patterns, my advice is to be open-minded about changing your responses. For instance, just because you may be a person who often gets angry or impatient in traffic or when kept waiting, doesn't mean you have to continue doing so. I often used to become very frustrated when waiting in queues, until I read a book that advised sending healing light and gratitude to people. I started practising this when waiting in line and things always went well, because no matter what the external situation was, I was feeling too peaceful for it to bother me. To help the line move faster I also think thoughts such as: 'The line moves easily; I am happy to be here; I may even run into somebody or experience serendipity because of the time this takes' (and I often have!). I use the time to think about anything I need or want to, whether it's remembering or planning or daydreaming. I send love and compassion to those around me and send understanding to others' frustration. I see that we are not separate; I have merely chosen to change my response. Again, the book *You can heal your life* by Louise L Hay is highly recommended here for help with changing your thinking and making better choices.

Another example: I was once at an intimate music concert where some university students were squashing me in and talking very loudly about toilets! They started grating on my nerves; their voices were right in my ear, I didn't have enough room to move, and I was getting too hot in a crowded room. In the past I would probably have overloaded and had to leave momentarily. But then I remembered that I control my own state, so I started using the method I have described above, adapting the thoughts to the situation, for instance: 'I am calm; I release the need to be annoyed; I have plenty of room to move'. Within a few minutes of me doing this, the conversation changed. The students started talking about *An Inconvenient Truth* and the environment. One of their friends with a very loud voice left and there was more room for me to move. In my own experience, when I am willing to change myself and my thinking, the external situations respond accordingly.

Chapter 15 – Pop music and sex selling

They say that art, and in this case music, can be an expression or reflection of the culture, the society that it exists within, just as it can be a way to react against the society it exists within. If this is true, what does modern popular music tell us about our society today?

Although I sometimes catch some genuine artists with genuine intentions, whose songs and video clips denote a genuine idea or send a positive message, I must say that an awful lot of (not all) pop music videos are no more and no less than soft porn set to music. A lot of it is about tits and arse (there's no simpler way to put it). It is there to titillate, but by no means is it there to inspire deep thought, or emotional understanding, or to invoke an idea. Yes, many people say, 'Music is for entertainment'. Yet, I know many people, myself included, who experience music emotionally. It is about how it makes us feel. One of the best examples of this emotional expression I believe is found in the original blues musicians, such as Bessie Smith, followed by the explosion of musical genius in the 1960s, seen in Jimi Hendrix and Janis Joplin; later again we see this genius of expression in Jeff Buckley, and other great singers from that era. Currently in Australia Katie Noonan, Ash Grunwald and Chris Cheney are excellent examples of great expression borne from passion and commitment to one's art.

The blues had developed from the oppression of Africans brought to America and enslaved. Their work songs and protest songs were filled with that burning desperation one may feel when oppressed; an urgent need to express, to hope, to reach out. Blues music and a lot of other music is about something that calls to us as emotional, sensitive and spiritual beings. Modern music seems very light on these qualities.

There were a lot of changes that occurred in the 1960s. There was the social reaction to Vietnam. The societies then had lived through two world wars; they had experienced the consequences of war, unlike the young modern Westerner of today who has very little idea of this kind of hardship. There was also the recognition that freedom of thought and the right to question, are tantamount to a healthy individual, and ultimately, to a healthy society. People fought for equal rights for all. But something went askew when we got to Feminism. Yes, I believe women deserve equal rights, pay, respect—I could go on—as every other human on the planet. But what has feminism *actually* brought women? Now women have the 'right' to show their skin, to wear next to nothing (it wasn't that long ago in Western history that it was considered taboo for women to expose even their ankles), to make a lot of money selling their bodies, on video clips, on TV, on billboards, on anything and everything! They have the 'right' to make porn, to be strippers, prostitutes, models, display pieces (of course this has been prevalent throughout the history of mankind, but perhaps not so blatantly obvious to all in society—via advertising—as it is today). Yes, women can choose not to do any of this kind of work, but as long as the jobs exist, there will be women to fill them. Can someone please explain to me how constantly having the image of a female arse in my face will make me feel empowered as a woman? How are women 'equal' to men if the main way any woman can get very, very rich in the short or long term, is by showing some skin? I know when I see the types of guys that check out women from head to toe in that leering way, that it's fairly probable they have seen masses of images of naked women in their life, and carry this image of all women within or close to the stereotype. Good for perving on, good for sex, but that's all. And we say we are no longer living in the Dark Ages.[114]

Feminism, for whatever positives, has only taken away a fundamental right of women; which is to not have their semi-naked form paraded everywhere explicitly as a sexual object.

The fact that men have such 'easy access' to strippers and prostitutes, not to mention the many sex shops and explicit porn videos and mags, makes one wonder if this doesn't contribute to the disrespect of women overall, creating many relationship difficulties within our society.

Now back to pop music. Regardless of the great popular acts that are out there, the whole pop scene is extremely

---

[114] In fact in olden times and across many cultures, the woman would choose her mate based on her primal sense of which male had the strongest genes for her, in order to preserve and develop the quality of the human race. Still today women are drawn—although they may not be aware of it—to men who provide the most suitable genealogy for child bearing. Yet the focus today is on the woman 'selling it' to attract the man and not the other way around! This makes no sense biologically, and is akin to 'working against' the betterment of the species as women have specifically been given that primal instinct to choose their mate. This is true for all species (with the odd exception) and we must remember humans fit this definition also.

corporate these days, and is a lot more about selling the 'product' than the individual artist and their music. And for all the joyous sentimentality we may feel about the pop songs we remember growing up, or listen to currently, there are many messages in pop music that are not healthy for society to consume. One example is the constant flood of love songs that encourage us to feel that there is a perfect someone out there who will make all our problems go away or there is someone out there that we can blame for all our problems. The message is either: 'It's your fault I feel this way, you did this to me', or, 'You're the only one who can fix me, I need you to make me happy'. This doesn't teach us to be responsible for ourselves but rather to be powerless or to love parasitically; yet this is the music most of us grow up on, and how ironic that we do often get so shocked when our significant 'others' don't fit into the perfect picture we've already mapped out for them! Until we rise above these kinds of ideas we won't actually be able to have healthy relationships. This message of the 'perfect other' is expressed to us through so many ways, yet its concept usually does more harm than good.

There are also the songs that impressionable girls would perceive as 'empowering', the ones that (essentially) say: 'You did this to me but I'm still hot and other men will want to fuck me'. The female pop artists, who we are meant to feel are *empowering* us as women, are still sexing it up, only farther emphasising the idea that: Yes, other men will want them, but only *because* they are behaving seductively. It teaches women that they must be sexy to get a man at all; not desirable unless showing their female form. And the guys that have all those hot, hot dancers on those hot, hot clips, are merely guys who can afford to pay for them. They are not 'king dicks', they are only men with money. It is tragic that the nasty side of rap music (which is now 'popular') is influencing many young men, who sing the lyrics that refer to women as only good for one thing, often with accompanying derogatory terms. Because young people can be most impressionable, having a strong need to feel secure, wanted, and to have an image, this kind of rap music easily turns boys into chauvinists before they get to experience the joy of getting to know a girl. It also teaches young girls that *only image matters.*

An example of the kind of negative messages we can receive through pop music can be found in Justin Timberlake's single *What goes around,* which I saw once on *Rage* (an Australian music TV program). During the film clip there is a mini-film. The whole story goes something like this: Timberlake says something like, 'Take care of my girl for me' to another guy while he himself goes towards another girl— girlfriend and other guy are found kissing—Timberlake goes nuts and punches the guy as well as being violent towards the girlfriend—girlfriend gets upset—both Timberlake and girlfriend speed off separately in very expensive cars—girl gets into accident—girl lies dead on ground—Timberlake stands over her while he continues singing: 'What goes around, what goes around, what goes around'. Considering that Justin Timberlake is always dancing with many different women on his clips, and this clip is no exception, this is obviously a glaring double-standard. This example farther perpetuates the old beliefs that: 'Men can be as sexual as they want with whoever they want, but any woman who does so is considered a slut', or, 'it's ok for women to be punished for infidelity, but not so for men'. And in many cultures men are the only ones making those decisions! Old thinking—new World.

At August 2007, there is a Bonds ad airing during prime time TV on Channel 10 that shows at least 20 young teenage girls in bras and knickers, showing just as much cleavage and arse as you'd expect to see on any underwear commercial, and as disgraceful as all that is, at least those models are over 18! What message does this send to young teenage girls, many of them probably watching *Neighbours?*

Young girls are dying of anorexia increasingly. *In these wealthy countries, young girls are starving themselves to death,* because of the pressure that comes from all this sexual imagery throughout our society. Doesn't this fact *alone* show you how unhealthy the society we live in actually is? And why do we hear day after day about various celebrities and their lives, yet never hear about how many young girls have died due to eating disorders?

Females, from as young as they can perceive images through TV and advertising, are subjected to this sexual imagery which fuels their insecurities, in turn creating the mass profits made from all beauty services and products.

For all these reasons, I see very little in pop music that is going to help human beings evolve in any way at all. If the use of music to sell sex is a reflection of our modern culture then we can view it in the same way as we do ads and TV; we are being asked to watch or buy based on our feelings of insecurity, fear, greed, envy, and sexual desire. Sexual desire is a wonderful beautiful thing when shared between individuals, but when they are beckoning it out of you through teasing and titillation; when it is constantly 'in your face', from the porn magazines in every convenience store, to the mainstream magazines and on television, to the pop video clips that you see on *Video Hits* and *Rage,* and all the 'get sex on your mobile' ads; our sexual desires are spread thin across all media, across all society.

Why is this so unhealthy? Because it desensitises us! It upholds the modern ideology that women are sex symbols (of course only those who fit the stereotype) and men are the desirers, who *should* be lapping it up, simply because they are men. We are constantly bombarded with sexual imagery and this fills us with a visual dialogue that may only make it harder for us to find our own personal sexual expression. An example of this is a girl acting what she sees as stereotypically 'sexy' because she thinks that's the way she's supposed to act to please a guy, and a guy having sex purely for gratification, to see the girl as 'sexy' with no emotional involvement. How many times have you heard the saying of: 'All men want is sex'? Even if this were true, aren't men still human beings in need of love, compassion and sensitivity? Don't men also need their partners to understand when they are not 'in the mood' for any reason? If a married guy is made an offer of sex with someone not his wife, it is often inferred in society (through mainstream media) that he won't be able to 'resist the urge'. Of course this can be true for some men but to say it is true for all men is just downright insulting. I'm sure there are many men throughout the world that deem love of much higher value than sex. There are also many men who don't just 'take what they need' from women, but rather support them in their own sexual expression. Since the feminist movement of the 60s, women have felt more confident in this area, which puts the sexes on a more equal footing and that is great, but it is not great if women feel that being sexual is the only thing that they are being valued for. It is no lie that sex can be highly pleasurable for both sexes. But physical sex only fulfils physical needs. As humans we have many other needs too—mental, emotional, and spiritual—and the fundamental need to express our own truth with others. *In true intimacy, all these factors are present.* It is when we share our hearts with others that we can experience the incredible feeling of love. Love takes care of all our needs. This is why I believe that men seeing women as extensions of their sexual organs, is incredibly unhealthy for both sexes (and true also if the roles are reversed). Men *create life* with their sexual organs; there is no more sacred act on earth. Women develop those life forms inside their own bodies. Sex is the entire reason that humans are able to procreate (though this is happening way too rapidly—give poor countries free contraception!). But all through our capitalist Western societies even the idea of sexuality—*our sacred life force*—is boxed, and sold to us the same way, over and over again.

Another great example of this is how many men (and women) learn how to have sex from watching porn? Yet the porn industry chiefly exploits women; predominantly the goal is focused on the males, and not the females, needs. Whoever learns about sex through this kind of pornography simply perpetuates the same old ideas. And so it goes on. Of course individuals and couples can make their own healthier choices, which are mutually empowering for themselves and their partners.

162

We must realise that most pop music and sex selling is not satisfying any of our core human needs, such as our need for true love and to express our true essence. The mainstream media projected throughout society encourages us to get shallower and shallower by the day; to be in fact *de*volving. Our current culture is impelling us to nurture our base emotions, the ones that present the least opportunity for spiritual growth, asking us to sell out our true nature and trade it in for a cheap fake copy. And as with other elements of society I have discussed, here again we are talking about an industry, the music/dance video industry, that is making billions of dollars every year. But does any of it enrich your soul?

I encourage you to search for and listen to music that makes you feel *something,* more than sexual titillation (as I'm sure many of you are). Go for music that helps you deal with life, not live in a shallow emotional state. Because the longer you live in a shallow emotional state, the more you may feel the need to find a substitute for life.

Chapter 16 – Drugs and alcohol

True well-being ultimately derives from an understanding of self. M.M.

In the long history of life on this planet there have grown plants that if processed in certain ways (i.e. opium to heroin), or left unprocessed (i.e. marijuana), and ingested in some form, have the ability to elevate human consciousness, expand the boundaries of the mind, make one very sick ... all depending on what was taken and how it was taken. Ancient and Indigenous cultures of the world have been known to have practiced enlightenment through the taking of such substances. It is important to note that through deprivation methods (such as of food, water, or sleep) similar experiences of enlightenment have occurred. Regardless of the method used, these quests for enlightenment were not random practices but rather done with reverence for the spiritual and universal mind (of course this would not be exactly true for every culture, but it is definitely true as a general rule for most cultures, particularly ancient and Indigenous cultures).

I am giving this background on what we now call 'drugs' as it is important to recognise that people in various cultures have practiced drug taking to farther explore the nature of life. But this was done as a spiritual practice; not for a cheap thrill. However, since most of the ancient and Indigenous cultures of the world have been colonised—hence destroyed[115]—we now

---

[115] In saying this I don't want to discount the importance of all those who have worked valiantly to protect their culture, as we are blessed by that.

have societies in the world taking drugs without the spiritual structures. Indeed, many people nowadays who do take drugs may have little idea of what they are searching for and may not be taking drugs to explore reality, but rather to escape from it. I am not saying this is true for every individual.

Looking at our recent history, we see that in the 1960s there was an explosion in the taking of acid and other mind-bending drugs. And, as discussed in the last chapter, there were important changes taking place in society; such as the political activism inspired by Vietnam, along with the Indigenous and women's rights movements. But over the following 40 years or so we slid back into conservatism, which is why we are now allowing the same terrible things to happen again, in Iraq. My point is, back in the 60s, the world was changing in radical ways and mass drug taking was an element of this, but people felt they were fighting for a better world, and I'm sure some of those people aligned drug taking with spiritual beliefs or developed spiritual beliefs through drug taking. The drugs of the 60s were also known for their purity in form, as oppose to the endless array of synthetic drugs that are being taken now. But the most addictive drugs are, and in this order: nicotine, heroin, cocaine and alcohol. In almost all parts of the world, two of these drugs are legal. And I believe these two drugs kill many more people than all the illegal drugs combined.

Currently in Australia and in many other countries, though many youth are now far more aware of environmental and world issues, a lot of people once they hit 18 do the bars and the drinking and the drugs. They are not fighting for a better society; they are falling for the trap that society has set up for them. Alcohol companies are another billion dollar industry and every beer you drink contributes to that. Let's just look at how our 'non-culture' is organised: Alcohol is illegal to drink until you turn 18 (here in Australia). OK, well everyone knows that the teenage years are the hardest to cope with, as hormones are going crazy and emotions run rampage. It's also a huge time for peer pressure. Teenagers are restricted everywhere they turn. 'You can't drink', 'You're too young to smoke', 'Do your homework', 'Don't be late for school', 'Make sure you're home by 9pm', 'No sex', etc. These are the messages that teenagers are constantly bombarded with. But what's the one thing most teenagers want to do more than anything else? REBEL!

The thrill of breaking the rules just makes the forbidden thing *even more exciting.* So cigarette and alcohol companies actually have a market in our youth. Definitely, a percentage of their sales are produced by under-ages. But do they care? Of course not! That's future billion dollar income we're talking here. I would just like to suggest that things are set up in such a way that we will have more drinkers and smokers because of all the rules than we would ever have without them. I believe the system is designed perfectly, through rules, and the temptation of breaking them, to set-up our young into nicotine and alcohol addictions that they never wanted and never asked for. And when they still have those addictions through their 20s and 30s and 40s and even into old age, they may realise that they can't just 'get rid of them' and that much of their life has been influenced by cigarette and alcohol companies. Their souls were purchased at a very young age, and the price, or the cost, *is so high.* They can develop cancer, suffer liver failure; their addictions can actually kill them. And in life they certainly won't feel good physically (making them crave alcohol or cigarettes even more); they may not be able to cope emotionally, therefore their relationships may suffer. *But did anyone ever ask these multi-billionaires what price they should pay for poisoning the masses???*

They are the only ones who get off scot-free. All the rest are left with these addictions wondering how the hell they're going to quit the cigarettes—the anti-smoking industry is making a lot of money too; either way 'they' win—or alcoholics always craving the next drink, trying to escape the pain of their own existence.

I pray you can see: *It's a set-up and we are all the victims*. How can you expect to quit alcohol when there is a bottle-shop every street you drive down? You can by using your own will. But it is so advertised, so socially acceptable, so outrageously bad for us to consume in big amounts, and so incredibly damaging to our relationships. When I think of every child abused in any way by their 'drunk' parent, when I think of every wife beaten by their 'drunk' husband, when I think of every brawl and violent death caused by 'drunk' men, and all the sexual abuse that has occurred by people who were 'too drunk'. I hope you can see how sick the society we have set up is. (This is without even mentioning the horrific damage alcohol has done to our Indigenous race, which has not had the genetic history to cope with it.)

If we had any culture at all, we wouldn't need to ban teenagers from anything, because the values taught through parental upbringing (a wine, or not, during dinner) and society (encouraging interest in art, life, love, politics, intelligence); healthy role models would be entrenched into the psyche enough that teenagers wouldn't feel they had anything to rebel against. For today's teenager to truly rebel they would need to be vegan, use only ethical products, be a non-drinker/non-smoker and be doing humanitarian work; the opposite being true conformity in this current age.

Increasingly, studies have shown the damage alcohol does to teenage brains, prompting the response that the introduction of alcohol should be done as late as possible.[116] My response to this is that even if you raise your children sensibly, our alcohol driven culture is set up to lure many into excessive consumption. Alcohol is an extremely addictive poison, a drug, and individuals of all upbringings can fall victim to this. Until our culture stops glorifying alcohol there will be little changed in the number of people found to consume it.

People who are moderate and healthy and sane would tend not to go out binge drinking every weekend. But how many of us in society are taught to be moderate? How many *can* be moderate? How many have established self-control to transcend their addictions? In reality, we have many people that feel they have been treated badly, abused, or 'ripped-off' by others, by the government, or by 'life'. And we have many people who just want to 'be cool' and 'fit in' no matter how well-off they are. Essentially, we have many people vulnerable to addiction; due to the Howard government

---

[116] ABC, *Catalyst*, television program, Australia, 9 August 2007.

they are increasing by the day. Yet for all the extremely nasty side effects of alcohol and cigarettes, you can buy them absolutely everywhere! And the government makes a tidy little sum on those taxes too.

But it gets worse. As many problems as we have with alcohol and cigarette addiction, now young people have to deal with the onslaught of hard drugs. Hard drugs have now become mainstream. This means if you are the teenager thinking about smoking a joint and looking for pot, now you could be the teenager easily offered speed or ecstasy. One may then be encouraged to 'graduate' to snorting, crushed pills or powders. Pot is a herb that although very dangerous to some, cannot kill instantly with direct use, as these other drugs can. My views on this are as follows:

From what I understood of the world back in the 1980s and early 90s, if you knew someone was doing pills or amphetamines, you would see them as pretty messed up. (Maybe lots of people could handle those addictions but I'd never met one.) I won't go into heroin (or ice) here because it is so incredibly addictive that most people can't do it regularly, and if they do, struggle to overcome it. I praise all those who have and send my love to those who haven't. I want to focus more on the modern trend of weekend ecstasy and/or amphetamine taking. People that work 9-5, are seen as moderate in society, but instead of going out for Friday night drinks, they now go out for Friday night drinks plus pills, often adding speed to keep them awake, and along with any other drugs they choose to take. I'm sure there are plenty of unemployed people or casual workers that take hard drugs too (although they may be money tight trying to keep up the habit, pills now cost around the same as a gram of pot, which radically normalises them). But some workers take amphetamines so that they can go out after a long day at work, rather than sleep. This is a good example of the pressure some may feel to 'fit in' (although that is not necessarily the sole reason for them doing it). I view ecstasy in particular as an extremely shallow drug. I am not saying all the people who take it are shallow or do not have a deep experience—of course each person has their own experience! The acid in the 60s, due to the development of LSD, may have helped to open up some people's minds perhaps, and even though still incredibly damaging, if not taken heavily, it could possibly bring expansion to the self, which then could be incorporated into the 'straight' self, for example, with the person becoming more communicative or open to new ideas etc; a similar process to the spiritual practices of some world cultures. I am not promoting drugs here because through transcendental meditation and alternate therapies, as well as the altered states of awareness attainable through deprivation methods, all this can be experienced naturally (so to speak). I'm saying that all that acid in the 60s may have helped people to leap out of societal rigidity, with many becoming more open-minded and social. Love became something seen as much more valid and important as a global force. Now there is nothing wrong with that idea.

Ecstasy, on the other hand, creates this state of love and openness for the time that it is taken (it was invented by a guy who used it to counsel married couples). It can then open people up to love more permanently perhaps, but generally once the effect of the drug is gone people continually feel they need to take it again to get to that expressive place. They are happy and expressing themselves when they're on ecstasy, but not so much if they just go out for a night drinking. If the only time one can open up is on a pill then that's a pretty big trap. (Perhaps some of you may think that this is incorrect, but as I have said from the very beginning, I can only give you my own reflections and observations.) What I know is this: The drug ecstasy releases serotonin from the brain, but once the pill wears off, that's it! Bye-bye serotonin. A positive state of mind can help keep serotonin levels up (and certain foods can boost levels, like corn for example), but messing with the chemicals that make us 'feel good' seems incredibly dangerous. Ecstasy, in the literal meaning of the word, is a state that can be experienced many ways naturally; through sex, relaxation, human touch, love, music, and any activity you truly enjoy. So to find a substitute for it seems strange if you ask me. It is hard enough dealing with nicotine and alcohol addictions, let alone stripping yourself of serotonin.

This is why I feel that ecstasy and other such calibre drugs, including alcohol, are only taking us farther away from our always present (though constantly suppressed) feelings of humanity and compassion. We need to encourage emotional expression in our everyday lives to make this world better. We need to be honest with those we love when we wake in the morning, and always. I believe if people were always honest and treated others with respect, we would continually enjoy loving relationships. In loving relationships, communication is always present, and that feeling of connection is more than enough to sustain people when they go out, and they would never need to do drugs or drink to have a great night. Any form of escapism or hiding from the truth is only denying our own divinity, the divinity and infinity of life itself. What keeps people awake, without drugs and alcohol, is human interest. I could stay awake for days if the conversation was good enough (although sleeping may be healthier!). Sharing our hopes, dreams, and fears, *this* is the essence that drives true relationships, that makes us feel open and loving and able to *be* loved. It is so important to tell people what's really going on, because often when we observe others' moods we assume that 'it's us', or we become confused. If we all shared our true feelings we would realise the misconception of separation; we would realise that we all suffer in similar ways. If we truly shared our thoughts, we would see that people are pretty much the same the world over. They don't like pain, but they love love. Isn't it obvious people? *We are meant to become a loving and enlightened race of beings!!* Why else would we yearn for love so much? And have been given these incredible hearts that are able *to* love? Each human, if given a choice, would choose love over pain. Therefore it makes perfect sense to me that we are meant to evolve into a loving and enlightened race of beings.

Drugs and alcohol are not the answer, love is.
Appreciation of all life: that is the true ecstasy.

Ideas and Solutions:

- The irony about drugs is that the less we intake of any drug whether its pot, alcohol, or heroin, the greater its effect. We actually need very little of any drug to get 'high' if we are well-rounded and healthy people. The problem is the more we take of any of these drugs, the more we need to get the same high which is when the heavy addictions and problems start. The answer is to do *anything* healthy, whether its soaking in a spa; getting a massage; having raw fruit and veg juices; gently exercising; drinking water; sleeping enough so that its fully replenishing; having a luxuriant bath; eating great food, particularly with toxin purges like garlic and chilli; cleansing drinks and teas (like green tea). Put any self-nurturing acts such as these into the repertoire of your daily routine, ideally combined with taking less of any drug—even if only a little less—whilst continuing to insert these healthy acts and this moves the issue away from being problem focused by bringing the focus to what's good. Any simple act of health gently reminds the dark side that the light is always there and can be taken in very small portions as needed. Spending time in nature is also so crucial to remind anyone with a drug habit that the beauty of nature is always there for them too, although they may need to continually immerse themselves in it for its healing to soak through; when one has deadened one's senses it does take time to re-awaken them. Bit by bit, that universal healing around and within us reminds us again and again of its existence, all we need to do is gently allow its presence in our lives, and drink it in, in however small doses we want at the time.

- It may be true that cutting down and effectively managing an addiction is as healing as quitting it entirely. Allowing yourself to manage it better builds your self-esteem and shows understanding to whatever it was that led you into addiction. People's self-worth can become so low, which is why I believe self-acceptance and compassion around the addiction—along with the suggestions above and a willingness to keep an addiction as a small or smaller portion of your day and week—may over time be a better cure than going cold turkey, as this may be too extreme for some addicts.

It's essential that people know they have the choice to completely release any addiction, yet in absence of doing so, pursuing healing is so important. It's not hypocritical to be an addict and seek healing (doing both good and bad), no matter what bad anyone does, working towards healing is always paramount.

Chapter 17 – Depression

Has anyone ever asked the question: What is at the root of the Western world's epidemic with depression?

Is it possible that you cannot live in a world where there is mass human suffering without this having an effect on you? That the rest of the world is somehow 'in tune' with this human suffering, and naturally enough many feel that there is something fundamentally wrong? And no amount of anti-depressants is going to fix that. Only World Peace could.

As you have read in previous chapters, I completely understand the natural pain and depression that is felt by people who have suffered from any form of abuse. I can only hope that people in this situation will seek avenues of healing. But even people who have experienced great healing may still experience strong emotions; they just have better ways to deal with them. There are many branches that can lead to depression; pain, sadness, guilt, anger. It is how we deal with these feelings that's important. Self-love[117] (and by no means do I mean narcissism) is the only way for any human to feel completely whole. And this takes work. My advice is:

Know Yourself. Be Yourself. Heal Yourself.

---

[117] To love oneself, in my view, is to recognise yourself as you would your own loved ones, and to love yourself as much as you love others. Love is love; it lives within us. Of course sometimes we need to put those we love first, but in fact this is putting ourselves first, as it is what we truly want (to love them). That does not mean we have to sacrifice ourselves for others; this usually does not work for the best of both parties, as loving yourself always will.

But often if you go to see a doctor about your emotional state the almost immediate question will be: 'Do you want some medication for that depression?'

The problem with anti-depressants is inherent in its title. *Anti*-depressant. The term anti- literally means 'against'. This equates to depression being labelled as 'wrong', an unnecessary suffering.

But what about necessary suffering?

We, as human beings, have a wide range of emotions that we can experience. In all that I have read about mental health or spiritual growth, it seems that expressing our emotions in healthy ways is the best way to cope with them. Sometimes it's important to just allow ourselves to *feel* what is going on, so that we can find out what the real issue is. Sharing our emotions and being honest with others; this helps us to work out the root causes, and clarify how we really feel.

We are all humans! We *all* have the capacity for feeling these emotions, wherever we are in the world, at any time, and for many different reasons. It is normal to feel depressed if you have suffered through a situation that has hurt you! There are many situations that could make a human feel depressed. Here are some:

Being hungry
Being yelled at
Being put down, being left out, being abused, being an abuser, family break up, loss of a loved one, physical illness, mental anguish, drug abuse, hangovers, hearing about tragedy, living in one, etc.

Pervading meaninglessness and consumerism in society can also lead to states of depression, especially for those that feel they can't engage with external activities; yet it is also true that too much engagement with entertainment and society 'hype' can lead to depression too. At the same time that we are being told that 'healing' is ok (i.e. through the exponential rise of counselling and Eastern healing methods in the West), we are also being told that 'it's ok to self-medicate' if one feels they are having trouble (in many cases both may be needed). This can obviously lead to confusion which is also an ingredient for depression!

I believe they label depression as the state where one is hindered by it to the degree that it prevents one from living a full and healthy life. And that's where the anti-depressants come in.

I believe anyone offered anti-depressants should also be provided with counselling and given access to different healing treatments. The main good of anti-depressants is that they can stabilise a person suffering in the time being, but it is not a long-term solution. I believe depression has a cause, I believe it is a natural human emotion and suppressing it does no more good than putting a lid on a jar that someone is screaming in. It must come hand in hand with some form of therapy. Sounds complicated? Not really. It would be as simple as adding into the school curricula simple lessons on the tools of psychoanalysis and healing techniques. That is, finding root causes—usually directly related to our parents and upbringing—looking at our own behavioural patterns, figuring out our hopes and dreams and making a plan to reach them, as well as working on our forgiveness, compassion and well-being, etc. For all those with depression right now whether medicated or not, I advise you to read every book on healing that you can (or even just one). Meditate. Think. Allow the emotion to be, maybe then you can allow it to pass.

There is also the issue of what is called a chemical imbalance. This can occur in people whose brain chemistry has been altered through the heavy use of medications (particularly for mental illness) or from excessive drug use, or in those who have a history of mental instability. But there is also the case of those who are healthy and living well who then find themselves feeling depressed a lot for no apparent reason. In this case I ask: Is there a reason? (Perhaps something they're not yet aware of?) If not, one must look at all the factors that could help to alleviate the condition, i.e. great food, healing and alternate therapies, fun and relaxation etc., and if this doesn't work, perhaps anti-depressants are the only way to stabilise those brain chemicals. But once taking the anti-depressants the new chemicals establish a routine and when one stops taking them time is needed for the natural brain chemicals to re-adjust, requiring patience. But you still gotta deal with how you feel.

Our emotions are there for a reason. I have been depressed in my life, at many different times for different reasons, but I have never accepted any doctor's offer of anti-depressants. Why? Because I believed it was better to accept those heavy emotions, knowing I was depressed for a reason. All I had to do was figure out what that reason was. I still approach feelings of depression in this way. As I sit around feeling bad I think and think and note my feelings, my reactions to certain thoughts, and ask myself: Where did that come from? Why does that still hurt? What's holding me back from happiness; from love; from my dreams? I think of those I love and wonder if there's anything I could do to assist them which may improve my self-worth. (Although I've learnt over time this usually only distracts me from my own healing.) And also, who in my circle of friends could I turn to and talk to? Am I resisting reaching out to someone close, and if so, why? Am I abusing anyone in any way including myself? If I'm hurting myself it makes a lot of sense that I would be depressed. I do a complete self-analysis whilst also seeking paths to healing. In this way no matter how depressed I am, I accept that I have to ride the waves of time until those feelings abate and during that time I try to figure out solutions so that I can create a brighter future where I'm able to deal with any negative emotions in a healthier way. Ok. So, this works for me. I accept my depression. It is as much a part of me as my anger or my passion. Call me crazy but I appreciate the emotion. As long as I'm feeling depressed I know there are more issues to work on. I accept the pain of the process; accept my faults. I ask for answers and with a lot of introspection involved, I generally get them. Again, I cannot speak for the grief some people may have experienced or for those with long-term and debilitative depression. I have been very lucky, as many of us have been, although one can never underestimate any one person's personal suffering, as each person is their own measure.

I am saying that every time I feel depressed, I welcome it as I know that if I accept it and go through it, it will pass when it's ready no matter how long that takes, and it enriches my life by forcing me to make things better.

Scott Peck explains this well in *The Road Less Travelled:*

> Problems call forth our courage and wisdom. It is only because of problems that we grow mentally and spiritually. When we desire to encourage the growth of the human spirit, we challenge and encourage the human capacity to solve problems, just as in school we deliberately set problems for our children to solve. It is through the pain of confronting and resolving problems that we learn. As Benjamin Franklin said, 'Those things that hurt, instruct.'[118]

Often from depression can come the greatest healing. Sometimes it can act as a break from the outer world which gives the inner world a chance to be acknowledged; it can serve as extra time where what really matters can be put into perspective, and come to the surface and be dealt with. I believe it is healthy to get some other things on the burner no matter how crap we are feeling so that at least there is something to enjoy, however small, once the depression fades. If you have been in a terrible situation and are in great pain, it may be that time is the only healer, unless you are open to receiving healing through Reiki, meditation, Tai Chi, spiritual work, receiving love from friends or family etc., and of course this still takes time, but the time taken to heal is a very important part of the process. For all those feeling depressed, if you are unwilling or unable to seek help externally, here are some questions you could ask yourself that may help you resolve/heal this pain, internally, by using your own will and brain.

---

[118] S Peck, *The Road Less Travelled,* Simon and Shuster, United States, 1978, p. 16.

How am I really feeling?

What could have caused this?

If I know the cause, what is stopping me from seeking healing?

If I am seeking healing, can I accept the process of working through the pain without constricting it to a time frame?

Do I get upset that I'm not healing quickly enough, and does that help me?

How can I better learn to accept myself whilst in the healing process?

Do I respect my own needs?

If I know I've ignored deep feelings of hurt, can I open myself to healing?

Do I have a sense of what the pain is about?

Is it something I'm not yet willing to look at?

Is it something I'm not ready to resolve, and if so, why aren't I ready to resolve it?

Can I accept myself now for taking the time that's needed before I can heal this issue?

Am I blaming myself?

Am I blaming someone or something else?

How long have I felt this way?

What are my hopes and dreams?

If I don't have any, what would I like to be my hopes and dreams?

What do I need right now to feel ok?

How can I get that?

If what I want is harmful, can I accept myself for that too and still be willing to change?

If not, why not?

Can I accept my faults along with my abilities?

How many ways can I bring love and joy into my life and focus on what I truly want?

Am I filled with anger and resentment for other people?

Do I need to forgive (let go of) the pain these people have caused me in order to get on with my life?

Do I allow people to love me, or do I shut them out because of fear?

Do I allow my own problems to cloud the love I could find in others?

Do I need to forgive myself?

How are all my relationships?

Do I let other people abuse me?

Do I abuse others?

How are my actions affecting people?

How are my actions affecting me?

In all this questioning it is essential not to berate yourself, but rather to be willing to observe your own experience. Understand that you are in this state for a reason, to give you the opportunity to really *see* the problem, exactly what it is, and why and how it came about. It is important to accept that everything you have been through brings you to this current moment. Even if you cannot resolve a situation now, this in no way means you won't be able to resolve it in the future. As a friend said to me once on the subject of addictions, 'It will leave when it's ready'. This is true of emotions too; we are never permanently our emotions. Emotions come and go; our permanence is that we are conscious and alive.

We cannot blame ourselves for being where we are; in every experience we can choose to regret, or to learn. By learning we can only make things better, if that is our desire. We can change a negative to a positive with a single change in attitude. Just understand that if you honour yourself in all situations, you can get better, and you more than likely will.

Imagine exactly what you want in life and do everything you can to reach those goals. Allow yourself to be helped along the way, and when you are able, allow yourself to help others. Reach out to people!!

There is a place in all of us that needs love and needs to give love.

That place is in everyone you know. Reach out by being honest yourself, willing to hear others, not just from your viewpoint, but also from theirs. Look to see where you may be projecting your beliefs and fears onto others. As soon as we turn to blame someone or something else for what we don't like in our lives, we are giving up our own responsibility to solve a problem that is uniquely ours to solve. No one else can fix our problems for us, and nor would we want them to, as then we're waiting around for them to fix it whilst still feeling miserable. No matter what we have been through at some point we must take positive actions to resolve our problems if we truly do want change.

The only way to gain control over our lives is to know that we are each responsible for our own actions, once we accept that, we can change ourselves and stop putting that burden onto others.

We are not here to drain each other. We are here to reflect each other to see ourselves from many viewpoints. Use depression to figure out everything and just what you *do* want to have a better life. Forgive yourself for the time it takes. *Grow with it and through it.* If you believe you need anti-depressants to do that, that's fine, so long as you actively figure out long-term solutions whilst on them, and wean yourself off them at a sensible pace when you feel you're ready.

Ideas and Solutions:

- Do not be afraid to seek answers and to seek healing. We have access to so many healing methods. The idea of having a Reiki or a Tai Chi master; a kinesiologist or a counsellor (to name a few), is that you do not have to go through this alone! You can put yourself in the position to heal the pain with love and support, at your own pace, in your own time and on your own terms. You can start Tai Chi or Yoga classes (which are well known for their healing benefits) for as little as $10 a session, even less in some cases.
- We, as humans, have great ability to figure out our own solutions. It is time for us to become empowered with this ability, because no matter how terrible we think our problems are, they would only be compounded if we were living through a war. We must become empowered with our ability to solve our own problems simply because we can.
- People suffering from mental illness suffer even more under the mental health care system. Electric shock treatment *is* common, over prescription *is* common. There are many barbaric practices for our disabled and mentally ill still in place (the treatment of people in some aged care facilities is also of great concern). My solution is to encourage all relevant institutions to implement essential growth fostering elements into their programs, such as good food,

safe environment, creative activities, minimal drug prescription, counselling and lots of Eastern healing methods. Of course they would need funding and support from federal and state governments to do this. This would create a much saner world for all of us.

- Again, I highly recommend the book *You can heal your life* (Hay) for all those seeking healing. It explains methods of self-healing which you can do simply by *thinking* better, about yourself, and about everything. In many cases of depression, the power of the person's mind in bringing them down with difficult thoughts lacking in hope can become extreme. The mind *is* a powerful influence in our lives, and we must work towards its healing by refusing any inner dialogue that leaves us feeling we have nowhere to turn; as self-love is always a cure that exists within us.

Chapter 18 – Judgment and hypocrisy

We want freedom of speech but we all talkin' at the same time
We say we want peace but nobody wants to change their own mind
So it goes on and on and on and on and on for a thousand years ...
What language are you tears?[119]

Many of us in the 1st World may spend time criticising others rather than improving ourselves. We can get bogged down in our own hypocrisy. The criticism we may have of others will tend to sound like the criticism we give ourselves, criticism that we probably heard (learnt) at a very young age and are still repeating and that's the *real* problem.[120] But being critical of others will not solve that. We need to accept that if others don't know what we know, it is up to them to learn, not up to us to enforce learning. Some people hang around those they feel the need to criticise; this is only distracting them from their own growth.

I have learnt some valuable lessons on judgment in recent years. You know when you feel strongly that you are right about something and then find out later that you were wrong? Yet you tenaciously want to hold onto your belief? I used to hold on; now I happily surrender knowing it is the only way I can learn more. We must be self-expanding, rather than self-limiting, beings. We must be willing to be wrong and therefore open to more truth. We need to see all points of view from all sides,

---

[119] Michael Franti & Spearhead, *Is Love Enough?,* 2006.
[120] See Hay, pp. 27-29., for some examples on this type of inner dialogue.

and still desire peace for everyone.

"Everybody wants to tell their neighbors how to live but nobody wants to listen to how they feel ... "[121]

I know some working people harshly judge welfare recipients. They have a strange presumption that people on welfare are 'living it up' or 'sitting on their arses'. Perhaps this is true of some, but let's be more realistic here. People who study or have a disability or are new to this country etc., *are* restricted with how much they can work. Without welfare they would probably be homeless; certainly they would be hungry. When people criticise the welfare system they tend to conveniently forget that after rent, food, and bills, not to mention other costs, such as transport and education, *no one* on welfare has barely enough money left over for a massage, or travel, or luxury items.

There are many in this country growing up with parents or a parent on welfare. Kids who never had a head start; struggling in a 1st World country. Many poor people do the best they can to ration and survive. Many others smoke and drink and don't eat properly, or have problems with domestic violence, or many other difficulties that prevent them from overcoming life's obstacles. Please do not think that it is easy for these people to support themselves or to change their lives, let alone work full-time. You cannot judge welfare recipients unless you can also say that you would be happy to see those people living on the streets.

The greatest hypocrisy in our country is supporting a

---

[121] Michael Franti & Spearhead, *Is Love Enough?*, 2006.

leader that not only violates human rights but leaves our own poor behind, whilst labelling Australia 'the lucky country' that has 'Aussie values'. We have many homeless people in Australia—the figure in Melbourne alone is well over 20 000—even though our economy is apparently booming. There are many who want to live their lives in peace, yet simultaneously support war. The people to judge are not our next door neighbours but people in positions of power (but seriously have an open discussion with the neighbours if you know they vote Liberal; it's that human rights thing).

Some judge those from other countries that have English as a second language but do they know how literate these people are in their first language? I'm sure a lot more literate than most Australians!

Some judge drug addicts or homeless people but can they imagine what that experience is like or how those people came to be in that position? Some judge what they cannot understand; perhaps they could if only they were willing to.

Some complain about the things that they are not willing to change, which only burdens those around them, who have their own burdens.

We all need to recognise our own hypocrisy. It is only when we do, that we will stop being hypocrites; because then we can consciously make the choice not to be. It's important to understand our contradictions rather than deny them, because we are made up of them. We need to accept a wide range of beliefs, and still be able to understand our own truth. We need to realise that we could all hold different opinions, stand on different patches of ground at different times, depending on our situation, but we're all standing on the same land: Earth.

As mentioned in previous chapters, however we were raised leaves us bound to our own conditioning and we judge others according to what our conditioning tells us, forgetting that if we were raised in a different way, we would be bound by different conditioning, and therefore hold different beliefs. Until we understand how we are conditioned and work through this, we may make many judgments about others. Without recognising that we are created from One source, and are all part of the Whole of Life itself, we greatly suffer from feelings of separation.

> All that interferes with the natural flow of compassion is the tendency to separate this indivisible wholeness into self and other. Whatever we are unwilling to accept as our own embodiment, we have to project outward onto an "objective" Universe, which is actually a creation of mind. Once it has been "othered" in this way, we judge it as good or bad, better than me or worse than me.[122]

How often do we find ourselves doing this? When we are judging another, we need to go take a look in the mirror and see who it is we are really judging. For if we constantly find fault in others we may be set in a pattern that has nothing to do with them but everything to do with us. Sometimes it's essential to give up or change self-imposed and self-limiting beliefs. We must do this in order to grow. I can expand on beliefs I already have, stretch them so wide that they could encompass all

---

[122] AN Ardagh, *Relaxing into clear seeing*, SelfXpress, California, 1998, p. 316.

beliefs, or I could give up a belief that basically makes me feel bad. We all think we know how to solve everybody else's problems, but it is up to us to solve our own problems.

A thriving hypocrisy in society at present is found in the charities that ask us to support the starving in our world. There are many such charities we can donate to but there is one striking fact:

If our government, along with other 1^(st) World countries, signed up to the proposal like the one advocated by Bono, donating .07 of its gdp[123] to those starving in the world, there would be no world hunger!

And why do people have to sign up, making an individual choice to donate? Instead of individuals paying $30 a month, why not get everyone paying $3 or even 3¢ a month? Even our own poor could afford that without starving themselves. How about you take the millions of billions and *trillions* of dollars made by American movies and use that money to end world hunger?

What more blatant the hypocrisy than Foxtel costing the same amount per month as it costs to sponsor a starving child. These are the types of choices on offer in the 'free' world.

Yet how can we ever truly be free if we are denying our own humanity?

---

[123] Gross Domestic Product.

We cannot be held responsible for others' actions, but we can be responsible for our own actions, for how we vote and for how we treat others. We can understand the serious effect our individual choices have on all of us.

I have one thing here to say about homosexuality: What consenting adults do behind closed doors is absolutely no one else's business.

When we feel compassion, by imagining being in a fellow human's position, it opens our hearts and minds to understanding *all* human dilemmas. To judge is to ask to be judged. We must be open to different viewpoints, and not be rigid about any opinion or idea except those which we feel deny or overlook the basic principles of humanity.

Chapter 19 – More on society

Before we head into my conclusions for this book (after the next chapter: Greed), I just want to generally comment on some other issues that are great barriers to our growth and our humanity.

Gossip

Why waste your time 'bitching' about other people, when you have no intention whatsoever of understanding their point of view, or helping them to improve by talking to them about their behaviour? All gossipers know that in their circle of friends or family they are being talked about behind their backs too. It is such a waste of effort people! And makes us lesser people. Try releasing your need to endlessly criticise others, and look at your own behaviour.

Corporations

Ok, well, let's just look at Coles; just one example. In Coles ads across Australia you'll see/hear the slogan, 'You'll love Coles'. Why? Because all Coles brand name products will be cheaper than any other brand. 'Coles' is the new 'no-name' (in fact I think because of this Coles has sent the no-name brands broke, as the big supermarkets now have their own self-titled no-name products which surely has a negative effect on the previous no-name companies). Yet, whilst competitive brand products are always more expensive, what about the fruit and veggies? Coles are packaging up the spinach, the tomatoes, etc., and selling them for $4 a pack! It used to cost under $10 to buy a full load of veggies from Coles just a few years ago; nowadays it's almost $10 just to buy 2 vegetable items! The competitive brand products at Coles are going up and up, so now it's virtually impossible for the poor to escape having every item in their house with the sticker proclaiming: 'You'll love Coles', only adding to the huge profits Coles already makes. If you aren't already aware of this, the Australian company Wesfarmers owns every Coles, K-mart and Target Australia wide, so is making absolutely extraordinary profits on top of having their own brand.

Markets are always the cheapest place for food and at least then we are supporting an individual's way of life rather than a multi-billion dollar corporation. It is important that we support our local businesses. We must force those corporations' prices down, so that the old ladies and others, who can only go to Coles (or any of their subsidiaries), aren't forced to pay a disgusting amount of money just to survive.

Corporations display great hypocrisy in their behaviour. A good example of this is the Ronald McDonald house. Yes, it is wonderful to support families of children with cancer. Of course! Yet McDonald's food has helped to create the epidemic of obesity and it also contains many other undesirable elements which could *lead* to cancer. The human damage caused by McDonalds creates the need for many other places of charity, especially ones with programs to help fight obesity.

Many corporations commit atrocious acts upon people and Mother Nature in the name of money. The sooner we, the people, force them to become accountable, the better.

Negative behaviour

In particular, I'm thinking about all the drivers, workers or people in general that respond to others' actions by saying, 'You bastard', or the like. The driving thing is like, here are heaps of individuals driving around *one person per car,* each fairly desperate to get home or to work, spending a lot of their driving time being frustrated by other drivers! But we all want to get home, or we all don't want to be late, and those who don't understand this are insulting each other. It's just not healthy. Let people in, courteously tell them the road rules if need be, but know that you can't understand the situation that other driver is in, unless you have great skills in empathy! We can get as frustrated as we want, but it just uses up energy that could be spent on better things. Use traffic time to muse and clear difficult thoughts by taking a few deep breaths and allowing some clarity for solutions to come to you; if you're going to be 'stuck' there, you may as well use the time productively. You can apply this to many situations. Just do the right thing by yourself and don't allow others' negative behaviour turn *you* into a negative person. Rather, come hang out with those of us who have hope.

Mindless Entertainment

Why is art and music prevalent in the entire human history of the world and in every culture of the world? What is it that separates us from the Apes and other animals, aside from less hair, greater mobility, and a larger brain? I believe it is our heightened sense of awareness, our critical thinking, and emotional reasoning that allows us to aesthetically experience the

194

world around us so deeply and which makes our existence so unique—but remember our genetic make-up is less than 1% in difference to the genetic make-up of Apes; we are a lot less different to our fellow life forms than many of us think.

We humans experience a great deal through sensory perceptions. The scent of a certain flower can return us to a childhood memory; listening to music can create a certain mood. Do you remember what it was like painting in art class in school? Or watching a sunset? Or what it feels like to sit with your eyes closed, no sounds or interference, just you and the quiet? We are human beings people! We were not given these amazing sensory perceptions so that we could literally slaughter them, rendering them senseless. All that loud meaningless music, all those blaring radio ads, all that ghastly commercial TV, all those roaring cars producing crappy air, all that 'go go go, no time to stop' attitude, all this takes us so far away from our basic right to live a life full of wonder, able to explore the depths of our very own nature, and in so doing develop great appreciation for life itself.

If you live in a city you will notice that even in the middle of the night there is a constant underlying hum. To achieve silence is difficult, but there is enough peace within our very own souls for us to experience tranquillity; all we have to do is listen.

Mobile phones

Now we can all be contacted, all the time. Sure helps us to have less time, because everything is becoming instant. I don't want to go on about mobiles here but I do want to say this—increase in nose, throat and mouth cancer; increase in brain tumours. They're still doing the research but having that many electromagnetic waves by your head cannot be good for the brain. Use them when you need to, and briefly. We will have a much better idea of this in the next 50 years. I predict that we will learn of some negative consequences. This also applies to TV and computer usage which, if excessive, I believe can diminish eyesight, overload the impulses, and effectively 'heat up' the brain.

There is that other insidious aspect of mobile phones; mobile assault.[124] I can only repeat that in a society that encourages immorality, this kind of behaviour is likely to increase. When sex, violence, stupidity and hypocrisy are sold everywhere, how do we expect our young or anyone easily influenced to make informed and humane judgments?

The Internet

Instant access; let's use this to communicate our humanity throughout the world. Forget about the entertainment or the 'peruse 'cause I wanna be amused' attitude, and go for the 'let us communicate for the greater good of all humanity' attitude. There is so much inhumane stuff on the net. There are some things you should never be able to put on the web. If I want to see something horrible I can watch SBS World News and see it for real. I do not choose to see horror, but do see the reality of horror in our world. Whatever I see is for the purposes of knowledge, not for amusement. But on

---

[124] I am referring to the recent trend of attackers filming their crimes on mobile phones.

196

the Internet, there are videos of all manner of the most inhumane crimes; even though there are laws against this it is happening anyway. We must fight to protect human dignity. Many of our young are technologically savvy and can access footage—even unwittingly—containing content that no one who isn't sadistic would want to see. People post stuff like this merely for entertainment, influencing others to think that this is acceptable. And if our young don't know any better, what happens then?

The upside to the Internet that I believe ultimately trumps its ills is the networking of people all across the globe, connecting with each other on common issues, such as global warming and advocating for human rights. It is so easy to sign an online petition or email members of government. This technology is the ultimate vehicle for the demonstration of global people power.

<u>The moral line</u>

You know, there is this whole, 'Let's keep them amused and immoral, that way they won't care what we do' thing. This is the message coming from the leaders of capitalism straight to you. If you can laugh at anything you may as well throw away human dignity too. Some things must be held as sacred; some things can never be joked about; some things must never be glorified, sensationalised, or trivialised; on the Internet, by people, on TV, and in society. For example: rape, murder, violence, child abuse, torture. All the things that we could never bear to suffer ourselves. Some things must be held as sacred. If we cannot be sensitive to human agony, we are surely doomed. (I make this point as it seems *some* 'comedy' shows are often going to the extreme which is extremely disconcerting; sadly I have not listed here any subject that I haven't seen to be 'satirised' in one way or another on a comedy show or by other human beings.)

The rich are only getting richer and the poor are only increasing; indoctrinating immorality is just one way to divert people from the truth of this; a sure-fire way to suppress the humanity of the masses.

Western Lifestyle

It is frightening that many of the privileged who are consuming, consuming, consuming, seem to have no comprehension of the greater issues at stake for the human race. And without the privileged being willing to give up some of the habits of their selfish lifestyles or to enact some kind of compassion, we have masses holding us back from our pursuit for human rights for all, not just for the privileged. Their consumption keeps the wheels of the capitalist system spinning; they are integral to maintaining it. We must remind them of the bigger picture whenever we can.

Do you know that approximately 90% of the people in the world are underprivileged, with 10% currently holding the world's wealth? And who comes into that 10%? Us! This is not right, this is not right. I, for one, am certainly not willing to indulge in my own monetary pursuits, just so I can drive around in a sports car flaunting my privilege. We must let go of our addictions to materialism. All we have to do is imagine what it would be like to have nothing.

And now our selfish greedy lifestyle is catching up with

us, due to our reckless use of resources. We are paying for the mistakes of the lifestyle we haven't questioned. Even though our parents could have done better, it is up to us to recognise and know that we *can* do better. *And we must.* It is time for us all to accept that every human interaction has an effect on the surrounding environment. It's time to truly appreciate how precious our environment is. And instead of exploiting it, protect it.

It is obvious that the more we stray from the simple life—air, water, food, shelter, love—the more needy, greedy, selfish, distracted, and inhumane we become. Meaninglessness, dulled senses, and numbness are all symptoms of our own refusal to take this existence seriously.

Ideas and Solutions:

- If you are feeling burnt out, tired, overworked, and stressed; if you feel any kind of lethargy or discontent; time in nature can be a powerful cure to help you re-energise, reinvigorate, and reconnect with your self. When we constantly have things on the go and are not doing any sort of replenishing, the simple acts of sitting by or hugging a tree; taking a walk in a park rich in greenery; splashing fresh water from a creek or river (or even the bathroom) on our faces; breathing deeply in the outdoors; and any other action that involves sharing in Mother Nature can truly be so wonderfully rejuvenating for mind, body and spirit. This can be easy to forget.

- Take the time to create even just 5 minutes a week where you sit in a quiet place of your home or any place where you can take some time out to relax, breathe, let go, unwind. Any form of relaxation or meditation is wonderful for strengthening yourself and brings you clarity which can greatly improve your state of mind.

- A very brief exercise of simply relaxing all areas of the face (using the method as shown in Ideas and Solutions, p. 119.) can show just how much tension we are holding and how much stress we need to release. There are a lot of meridian points on the face so this is an excellent exercise just on its own.

- Tune into everything that you feel is real, potent, natural, magical, and special to you. The more you allow yourself to indulge in and enjoy these energies the more you increase your capacity to accept and *embody* these qualities into your life.

Chapter 20 – Greed

If there is one human trait that could lead to the destruction of all things, it would have to be greed. M.M.

I started with guilt and end with greed; in my opinion the vilest of human conditions. I know that we can all hurt each other in our own ways but it's the greedy that are hurting a lot of people in a lot of ways. Greed is the cause of every invasion in the history of the world. Greed is the reason our precious, sacred, glorious and gracious world is being ripped to pieces. Greed, since the beginning of man, has taken bread from the poor, starved billions of people, killed, raped, stolen, broken so many and so much. Greed occurs in human beings who end up ripping off many other humans who could not be greedy to save themselves.

Greed rips up our Mother Earth and sells, sells, sells it. Greed doesn't care if the planet is destroyed, just so long as the back pocket can be filled up now. The greedy human will happily shed their humanity if it means they can get richer. And they always do.

Remember all the pubs we used to have when it was just your cigarette and alcohol corporations getting all the money and the government getting all their taxes? But then Jeff Kennet[125] (Liberal Victorian Premier: 1990s)

---

[125] How sickeningly ironic that Jeff Kennet is the director of *Beyond Blue,* when his actions as premier involved shutting down public schools, hospitals and mental health care services, as well as his implementation of increasing gambling venues, all of which has created a climate for depression which is still having a terrible effect on many Victorians today!

went and got Melbourne a casino and brought in the pokies, real pokies, not just the little number games you might find in a lonely pub, but fancy games, 100s of machines, spreading like a contagion through hotels everywhere. Many of those old hotels are now gaming venues.

A friend of mine mentioned a little story to me recently, something like, 'There's this guy I know, he runs a pokies place he does, and he reckons he's making a very tidy sum. He's paid off his house, got a $50 000 car, yeah he's doing alright'.

And I replied to my friend, 'I wonder how that guy feels seeing the same 80 year old lady gambling week after week, spending all her pension, and noticing the big shiny rings she used to wear aren't on her fingers anymore? Does he understand that this woman would never be playing the pokies if one wasn't by her local shops? Does that rich man ever look at her and feel any responsibility or regret for her state of affairs? I wonder; how does that man turn off his humanity?'

One thing greed will do is cause a human to justify inhumane actions and deny all charges against him/her, to protect or farther their cause. You would have heard the greedy talk before, and the greedy party in justifying their actions will say something to the effect of:

'But I never forced that old lady to play the pokies. It's not my responsibility what other people do. Besides, she's probably lonely anyway so I'm actually creating a good environment for her to get out and about.' (Sound like anyone?)

Now this is a hypocritical response for two reasons:

A: Human beings are not invulnerable to addictions, such as gambling, this is what we know. Therefore creating an environment that supports it is bound to catch many victims. Sure, some people can control it and have fun. Others won't eat for a week or will lose their homes along with incurring many other nasty consequences, such as guilt, family breakdown, bankruptcy etc. In lieu of this it seems quite inhumane to erect so many gambling establishments. Add up all those victims and you're looking at a lot of broken lives, which in turn affects the surrounding society. So how can all these pokies ever be justified, knowing that we have no control over people's vulnerability to gambling addictions?

B: If a pokies owner really cared about an older person's need for community and activity, they wouldn't run a pokies venue, they would run a community centre that ran activities and was a safe place for that older person to go.

As I have said, a greedy person will say anything they have to, to justify inhumane behaviour. John Howard does it all the time, along with many other 'leaders'. The greedy are only the leaders of destruction.

Where is the greed in you? What do you do with it? If you choose greed you have to trade in a few things, like honesty, healthy relationships, love, truth, compassion, humanity and so on. Love cannot live where one only wants to take and never to give. It just creates a big wall that shuts out the rest of the human race. Greed replaces love in its human host and then changes it to ambition and desire. Love for money is only the desire *for* money. Love springs from the depths of our beings and can never be bought or sold or taken or traded. But once desire replaces actual love, then it's bye-bye compassion, bye-bye humanity. Hello lots of money $$$$$$$$s.

Isn't it interesting how those who share the most tend to be the poorest? Is it that the more we have, the less we realise just how much we have? And the more we lose the concept of what having nothing means? To have very little places great value on having anything at all, where as excess is so excessive. So many of us have so much we don't know what to do with half the stuff! But less is more. The simple life is more peaceful. We should only have that which we need, that which brings us peace, or closer to our life's dream. To resonate with what we truly love will always have a positive effect. If that dream involves money and expenses, we need to balance it out by contributing to our surrounding community in meaningful, as well as material, ways.

It seems that most people who are busy working to secure food and shelter don't get time to be greedy; they are too busy paying bills! If they don't keep working they cannot secure their food and shelter. As a friend said to me recently, 'the average Australian is only one pay check away from losing their home', meaning if they weren't paid, one more missed mortgage payment is all it would take. And it seems in many cases, all those workers are getting ripped off by someone greedy. This situation is no more obvious than in the exploitation of slaves by some greedy inhuman human who 'just wants to make a profit' and says, 'the less I pay them the more I make', and, 'then I can impress all my family and friends with my new brand of coffee cups and be so generous to them by giving them my wares cheaply because I made this great product and as for those poor starving, any wage is good for them! We are all happy and well!'

If you're generous to others, whilst you're ripping somebody else off, well, that doesn't make you generous at all.

The more the greedy have, the more they want. We are in urgent need of a cure.

Not only do we need to counteract and thoroughly deal with our own greedy tendencies, we urgently need to express our humanity to the greedy. We need to communicate to them through all possible channels (the Internet, music, TV, letters, articles, books, discussions) and express our utter disgust at their inhumaneness. If millions of us did this we may just force them into, at the very least, sharing their incredible wealth with those most desperate.

Perhaps we collectively need to send the movie industry broke, unless they donate a percentage of earnings to charity. *How can a single Hollywood actor earn the sum of 20 million or more per film, whilst way over 20 million people live on less than a $1 a day?* It is essentially the masses that can afford a movie ticket, that are 'greedy' for entertainment, who are supporting this insane inhumane reality.

The only reason war exists is because people benefit from it, regardless of who suffers for them to benefit. If we truly want peace in this world, we must be willing to forego our selfishness; as individuals, as countries, as the human race.

We urgently need to communicate this with each other and realise that *we are not alone!* We are *all* being controlled by the greedy in one way or another. They own everything. If they could, they would privatise and sell our entire world. Did I say could? Better change that to, they *are* privatising and selling our entire world. Even our human genes are patented, leaving the study of cures, cloning, and other medical research in the hands of very few people, only available to those who can afford to pay for the rights of using them.

If you do care, by Goddess you can do a lot. Remember, we control them, once we stop consuming. We control them. Who needs money anyway? Whose stupid idea was that?

If we were an enlightened race of beings, living by the rules of humanity, with our God being accepted as every single cell in our sacred Universe (how could a God be anything less?) do you really think we could abide by living with money?

Money buys stuff. It can be made out of plastic, or copper, or paper, and so on; so, what, this is what buys my right to food, energy and water? But hang on, didn't our master Mother Earth provide all this for us anyway? Then what do I need money for? When did someone say, 'You can buy that'?? How can you buy water? It's utterly insane. Apparently quite a few villages in the world have had their water 'bought' and privatised. Yeah, and now they have to pay for their own water, oh, but of course most can't afford it, so are forced to drink unsanitary water instead and *its killing them!*

Many rich folk hold strong judgments about poor people, seeing them as 'not strong enough, therefore not deserving'. Rather than the 'survival of the fittest' idea, where only the strong survive, these days it's more accurately the 'survival of the richest'. The only way the rich could know if they were ever really 'better' or 'stronger' than the poor, would be to strip themselves of all money and possessions and go live in Burma for a year.

Oh Man, Oh Greed, you woeful pathetic creatures. You Gollums, you dictators, you corporate billionaires. Wouldn't investing money into feeding a starving nation reward you more than anything else in the whole wide world? Oh that's right; you're exploiting those nations so that you can get unfathomably rich. Greed has always caused many innocent people unfathomable suffering and it … still … is.

People who heal their greed become healers and humanitarian workers; they become compassionate people. People who are consumed by it become dictators and billionaires. It is the choices that we make that lead us down either one of these roads. The lesson is to choose *not* to be greedy, *not* to be selfish, in any situation, and not to allow others to be so with you.

PART THREE – Where do we go from here?

Chapter 21 – Conscious awareness

Ever since I was young, I have felt huge compassion towards my fellow human beings and a fundamental sense that humans are not meant to be living with such mass suffering and oppression as they are. When I heard of the starvation in Ethiopia as a child, I would think of what it felt like when I was hungry just waiting for dinner and imagined how bad that would be after days or weeks without food. Even if we cannot relate to this personally, it is through imagining another's experience that we develop empathy. I have always felt a huge urge to do what I could to somehow heal the world and people in it, but I had to become consciously aware first.

In the past, I was aware that some people seemed to treat me well and others didn't. If they didn't I would feel very hurt. I was insecure and others' hurtful behaviour only emphasised that. The difference today is that I now *know* that no matter how other people behave, it is up to me to take care of myself. The best way for me to do this is to understand and honour my feelings and leave situations I am unhappy in. In terms of maintaining my self-esteem, I can now see that others' behaviour often relates to their own issues; not to mine! And I have learnt that the best way to love others is to *not accept* their hurtful behaviour!! If one does feel they are being treated badly, at all costs one must fight for their own rights. People who act cruelly towards others are only depriving themselves of love; by hurting others they are not allowing themselves to *be* loved. This is a dire outcome for all parties. I believe the problems we have in human relationships are created by

208

our lack of total honesty with ourselves and with our loved ones. We are too busy wearing masks and/or reacting to our own conditioning. There are many people hurting each other, emotionally, and in many ways. And over the years of observing myself and my fellow humans, I can tell you that we all need conscious awareness because we are all choosing.

I know a lot of people who hurt others are riddled with guilt (which only perpetuates the negative behaviour) or they are just not aware. Perhaps they are being cruel deliberately.

If people were aware that they had a choice in every human interaction, do you think they would behave as badly as some do?

Some people think that they are aware and may say things like: 'Yeah, I'm a bitch, but my friends know that', or, 'Yeah, I'm an arsehole, but you gotta be in this world otherwise people will fuck you over'.

These are two reasonably common beliefs that I have heard over the years from both sexes.

Being hard and tough in order to not get hurt is ok for a while, but not forever, because if you don't let anybody else in, you miss the experience of truly sharing your heart with others in the incredible way we have been given as humans to share, through love.

Being proud of being a 'bitch' is nothing to be proud of, it is merely a form of self-protection, of always having to be right; a way of shutting out love.

As long as people are shutting out love in an attempt to protect themselves, their love remains locked away from the world. There is so much love left unshared, but just because it has been that way, doesn't mean it has to still be that way. As soon as you are safe, there is nothing that should hold you back from love. To love is to care about the spiritual growth of yourself, those you love, and every human being. To love is to appreciate life itself. To spiritually grow, or to be consciously aware, we need love and support from ourselves and from others. I believe that if we embraced these values we would all contribute to the greater good.

Now, as a child, this fundamental wrong I felt—and still feel—about humankind came from two specific things I learnt in primary school:

1) That although there was plenty of money in certain countries of the world, millions of others were starving and dying from preventable diseases, etc.
2) That the English came here and slaughtered the Indigenous population, used them as worker slaves, then tried to 'assimilate' them into white society with no recognition of the injustices, etc.

These facts about humanity and the country I was born in reinforced my deepest inner knowing, that human suffering is a terrible thing, which should never be inflicted upon any human being. And those human beings, who participate in acts of great cruelty towards others, are human beings making a choice. In the case where one is forced to commit a crime or be killed, one obviously has very few choices, but certainly a choice is made by those who command them.

So then the issue becomes not so much what to do about the humanitarian crises in the world, but what to do about human choices.

In the past, when I felt my life was difficult, sometimes I felt I was the only one with problems. I went about in public with what I'd call a 'chip on my shoulder'. I remember acting very grumpy to strangers or getting stressed at them if I was in a hurry. It took me a long time to realise that everything I do has an effect on people. I was not consciously aware of the feelings of people around me or of the situations they were in. I was already biased towards the idea that they weren't suffering as much as me, even though I understood generally that there are always people better or worse off. Anyway, here are a couple of incidents that were among many that rapidly changed my thinking and caused me to become self-aware.

I was off to work one day and not feeling very happy at all. Someone brushed past me in a rush and in that moment of human contact I felt a strong harshness; the feeling of a stranger brushing past me felt unbearable. I realised then that all the times I had barged to get to the train door first, or to get off first, that I was possibly hurting people. I thought about the worst-case scenario, of a person contemplating suicide; if they were at a train station and someone harshly brushed past them, that negative human contact might be just enough to push them over the edge. I learnt from that moment on that just because I was in a great hurry (which was obviously to do with my own time management issues; I was creating my own stress), didn't give me the right to act brashly around strangers. Conversely, I would always be the first to help a mother with a pram, or help others in need, but that still doesn't justify bad behaviour.

Another incident was with the local shop owner (where I lived many years ago). She was of Asian descent, and I only point this out because traditionally these people work very, very hard; working long hours, with no holidays, etc., and this shopkeeper was no exception. I used to go into this shop regularly, and more often than not, in a filthy mood (usually hung-over). When I bought chocolate there, I would always check the dates, because I had been burnt from so many shops before with out of date products (the inane woes of Western lifestyle). One day I went in and was looking through the caramello koala dates, when the woman became absolutely irate. She came around to the caramello koalas and started rifling through them in a rage. She was screaming about the dates, telling me she, 'always checks the dates and I come in every time, looking, searching for in date items, but they are all in date. I check, always check them', and so on. She was really very upset. I was immediately contrite, expressed apologies, and left the shop abruptly. From then on I was always very courteous to her and we ended up having a lovely relationship. I had learnt my lesson. And completely contrary to my belief, she tried very hard to keep items in date!

My point is that every single human interaction has an effect. And in relation to the choices that we make, we are often blinded to the fact that we are able to choose at all.

On the micro level, it is essential that we understand this truth in relation to our own lives. We have a profound effect on those around us. We can choose to be loving

212

towards others and ourselves. We can choose to be kind instead of cruel.

On the macro level, the people in positions of power are making choices. They have a profound effect on the people and the environment around them. They can choose to develop compassion for others. They can choose to be kind instead of cruel.

Do you think that the leader of a country, who, along with their government, isn't aware of the oppression they are inflicting onto the people of that country? Or the oppression they inflict on other countries? Do you think that Howard, Bush and Blair aren't consciously aware of world poverty and world destruction?

Of course they are!!

They are in positions of *power* and they wield that power over human beings! They aren't struggling for money or oppressed themselves. They have lived lives of great luxury and had all their education paid for. They come from conservative homes; they are moulded mentally by their upbringing and the beliefs inherent in conservatism. They have never lived one day on the streets. I am not saying that they have not suffered, because I do not know. But I can say that they are in positions of power where their choices are not based on having lived a hard life. Or maybe they have. It would be hard to shut off all the compassion in your heart, just because you have to have power, just because you have to be right. Perhaps on a greater scale, they are suffering very deeply, because the conservative beliefs that they have held onto for so long are creating tragedy and pain the world over.

*"Those who start wars never fight them and
Those who fight wars never like them"*[126]

Those in power are distanced from the horrific realities of the violence they enforce, not just on their enemies, but on their own soldiers, and in many cases around the world, on their own citizens. That's a heavy thing to live with but it is what they are choosing.

The essential problem is the people in power who are making this choice to kill, starve and oppress others, and all those who support them in doing so.

If you want to change the world for the better, you first have to change yourself for the better. The entire world is a reflection of what's in every human's head, all our capabilities, all our self-destructiveness, all our strengths and all our weaknesses. The best way to improve the situation is to become consciously aware of everything you do and the effect it has on everything around you.

We cannot change the current choices of the right-wing governments in the world but we can consciously choose to vote them out of power in our own country. We can vote only for governments that support human and environmental rights. I know there are many flaws in the current political systems, and this is a problem. But one thing at a time. At the very least, do not vote for leaders that support war, and if they do, ask that they be stood down. Do not vote for governments that lock up children and ignore their Indigenous populations. At the very least, vote Greens.

---

[126] Michael Franti & Spearhead, *Time to Go Home,* 2006.

Again, I am not saying I have all the answers but I do know some basic truths.

Human beings have the ability to evolve. We are *always* evolving. Yet in many ways we aren't evolving at all although we have great potential to. I know there are many people in the world who care about human rights. There are many humanitarian workers and documentary workers, often risking their lives to help others or to show us what is happening. There are healers the world over such as guides, carers and teachers; people that are helping others to restore themselves, to grow, to become self-aware, to reach their goals. There are many people all over doing this kind of work.

There are also many people with their heads in the clouds. People who choose to avoid life through escapism. People who don't want to deal with the problem. I say to these people: You can never truly know what it means to be human, unless you can share your love and passion with yourself and with the world. Clear the clouds, look at the world around you, and instead of seeing how it could hurt you, or what you could take from it, look at how you could change it for the better.

There are people so caught up in their pain, they cannot see the pain they are inflicting on themselves and others. I say to these people: I am so sorry for the terrible things you have been forced to experience, but don't let that destroy all your future. From this moment on you can choose to love instead of hate, yourself and others. You have the great power of choosing whether to perpetuate the pain, or to annul it completely. You can choose to let go of the past. See what you can do *right now* that would benefit yourself or the world in a positive way. See the incredible power you have to make your life wonderful or terrible. Know that you can find love forever, inside your very own heart, just by beginning to treat yourself the way you know, deep down inside, humans are meant to be treated.

To the people that deliberately cause pain, or maliciously try to dog down others, or stir up trouble, or who just outright insult, incite, demean, etc. I say to you: Why? Have you really been hurt that much, or have you been hurt at all? Does it really feel good to hurt another human being? Do you love yourself (treat yourself with respect and care)? Do you really want to make things harder for those around you? Do you know that you can choose to stop hurting people? All you have to do, next time you're in a position to hurt someone, is don't. If you don't think you can stop, travel far, far away into the serenity of a forest or to any place in nature and think deeply about the sort of life you're creating. Is it really worth creating so much destruction? Can you accept hurting others even if they can come to a place of healing? Can *you* come to a place of healing? All you have to do is to be *willing* to heal. Believe that there is a better way, a way where you can be loved. You have the power to make life wonderful or terrible, why not try choosing the former?

Howard could choose right now to withdraw troops from Iraq. It would decrease the threat of a terrorist attack, because unlike what some people may believe, terrorists are not trying to destroy our way of life. It is all such nonsense. Some terrorists or suicide bombers may want one thing, which is to *have* a way of life.

216

Even if this costs them their own lives, they believe it is the only way they can help the people they leave behind. I'm not saying I agree with their choice, but we can't say ourselves what we would do unless we were in their situation. You will find that when people are free to create peace, they are not setting up terrorist groups. Many terrorists have been created through America's oppressive tactics in Afghanistan, Iraq, Palestine (the U.S. are heavily involved in the Israeli occupation), and many other places in the world. America has its own reasons for wanting to control the Middle East; it has nothing to do with 'liberating' Middle Eastern countries, as thoroughly outlined in the first section of this book. They don't care about the people *at all;* they are brutal, they are despicable and they are intent on their goals. But at any moment America could choose to end all the madness.

But you look at a case like Darfur. Yes, if you have money, resources and troops holy God, get them there! Stop the groups that are committing atrocities. Protect the helpless. Send food, lots of food. Send clothes. Assess what people need and by Christ, get it there! There are many other places that need your help too. America, if you cared about human rights at all, you would use your power for good, not evil! Rather than fulfilling your own needs, you could feel great satisfaction by ending human misery! You could depose the very fascists you put into power, the fascists that serve your needs, by accepting that you can never justify mass slaughter, starvation, exploitation or oppression of people for your own personal gain, or for any reason. You have the power to make life wonderful for people, or terrible! Why do you choose the latter? Why is money, greed and power the only things that satisfy you? Why aren't you a saviour to people who need you, rather than a brutaliser to those who don't? Why are you the leaders that destroy the world, when you could choose to heal it?

Chapter 22 – Global warming

*It's a hot night, and it's getting hotter, the sun's drying
everything out
The ice caps are melting, have you not yet figured it out?
It's the state of the world, but you are part of this world
Don't ever underestimate the power you have to give or to
take*[127]

The forests are being decimated, the ice caps are melting, 'natural' catastrophes are occurring more than ever and it is getting hotter and hotter. The irregular weather patterns of El Nino, producing dry weather patterns, i.e. droughts, and La Nina, bringing wet weather patterns, i.e. floods, are striking with ever increasing ferocity and are a sign of the current instability in our climate. Not enough rain, too much rain, making it very hard to grow anything. But what is being done about it? Look at the current attitude towards energy. The capitalist countries are only interested in one thing: profit. Yes, renewable energy will cost more at the outset, most change does, but once enough people have taken to it, it becomes cheaper. Of course, the new should be integrated with the old until we can 'wean off' the old, and energy becomes completely new. And if we do this, we have the enormous benefit of being able to halt the mass destruction we are inflicting upon our environment and atmosphere.

When we talk about global warming it is important to rely on our own logic when processing all the information we hear on the subject. For example, if you

---

[127] Jess Hieser, *Change from within,* unreleased music single, Jess Hieser, 2007.

dig coal out of the earth in mass quantities, burn it, producing black smoke that is full of chemicals we *know* are deadly to humans if breathed in directly, isn't it obvious that this will kill other life forms too? The same thing applies to radiation; every time nuclear testing or uranium mining takes place (and it has in our own country for over 50 years), the poison in the water and ground then spreads, contaminating the birds, the fish, and of course, the people. Our Indigenous people are all too aware of this terrible situation. With a little research you will see that this is an ongoing issue; uranium bi-products continue to kill long after one has been exposed.

When forests the size of a thousand football fields are logged on a daily basis, the entire ecosystem is affected. Trees consume carbon dioxide and breathe out oxygen; the more we log, the more we are ultimately cutting off our own air supply. When you put this and the above points together, you see that not only are we putting poison into the air, which gets trapped in our atmosphere, we are also diminishing the one carbon reducing tool that we have. When the trees aren't taking in the carbon dioxide, the ocean and the ground is. When the ocean gets too hot it affects all marine life and melts the Arctic ice caps; the hotter it gets both in and out of the ocean, the more the sea rises. You can see where this will ultimately lead us: under water.

I make these points based purely on the logic of cause and effect. What we do to harm the earth ultimately harms us. We *know* the ice caps are melting; we *know* the coral reefs are dying. *These are not events which can be reversed!!* We can halt them at best. If we use our brains, it will become clear that not only must we cease our own personal destruction of the planet, we must also mobilise society in demanding that our governments and corporations do the same. There are many things we can do.[128]

The fact is, we have all the capabilities to heal the planet, we are just choosing not to! Howard is one of the greatest flouters of new energy incentives with his policies that suit his business agenda, but not the long-term agenda of the planet. We are considered backward internationally in our approach to global warming yet we have many, many new technologies that would solve this problem. Why isn't it mandatory for every new home to be built with solar panels, with the government subsidising the costs? Why aren't renewable sources being used to run our public transport systems? Why are big businesses allowed to mass pollute to the detriment of all human beings? These are questions we all know the answer to:

Money.

The whole oil crisis is so ironic when you look at the huge array of alternatives that could successfully be used to satisfy our energy needs. We are living in the 21st century people! Water can be used to run cars. Solar panels can be used to run cars. This is a huge subject and one of which I am by no means an authority, but I can tell you, there are a lot of unexplored options into viable safe technologies that have just as much capability of sustaining our needs as depleting the entire planet's natural resources.

---

[128] Joining the Get-Up campaign (Australia) or other similar organisations, like Friends of the Earth, is a good start.

Do you understand that we would not need the wars in Afghanistan and Iraq had we funded renewable energy in the last 30, or even 10 years? We could be self-sufficient for energy without exploiting other countries, always having disastrous effects on their citizens.

There are many islands in the world where the ocean is rising at a rate of 2.5cm a year! Those islands are literally disappearing, leaving many thousands displaced. The consequences of global warming may seem small to those who are comfortable, but its effects on our fellow human beings are diabolical.

It is obvious to many throughout the world, who have experienced the effects of global warming personally, that this is not a subject to be 'debated'. This is a real and unimaginable reality. For example: What else happens when the ocean heats up? There is an increase in fierce weather patterns, affecting weather worldwide. What happens when the coral reefs die; when more than 90% of the oceans big fish no longer exist? The ecosystems of the oceans are out of balance, just as we—humans—are out of balance with the land and sea.

This reality is certainly not one that should be denied. It is the entire future of our species, of our World, that is at stake.

There is much you can do in your own life to reduce your personal damage to the planet. Recycling, water saving, reduced car use, etc. But ultimately the biggest polluters are the corporations perpetuating the problem for 'profit' (solution: don't use their products), and the politicians who support them to their own benefit. We must vote for a government who will take this issue seriously. And it is very serious indeed. According to many scientists, if we do not get a grip on this situation within the next 10 years, and that number is closing rapidly, we may lose our grip altogether. If the current trend continues we are looking at diabolical consequences for us all. We must act NOW if we are to have a chance of turning this reality around. Instead of destroying our planet, we must make the choice to heal it.

Ideas and Solutions:

- Be aware that every person *does* make a difference.
- Care about creating a positive difference in everything you do.
- Watch Al Gore's *An Inconvenient Truth*. He may not be a saint, but I do believe he is doing some good here. The work of both David Suzuki and Peter Singer is also highly recommended.
- If we truly wanted a democratic Australia, it would be viable for a leader, such as John Howard, to run government alongside an Indigenous Elder. I can just imagine the conversations:

John Howard: 'Now, we got to sign this contract to expand our coal fire stations, and here's another one to continue mining uranium. So if you can just, ah, put your signature here … '

Elder: 'You cannot hurt the land.'

Howard: 'Oh well, but we have to, we've got

investors, we've got buyers, we can't upset
China, now let's not be hasty on this. Ah, what
if I employ some of your people, get them on
the projects?'

Elder: 'You cannot hurt the land.'

Chapter 23 – Creating the Universe

Know yourself and you shall know your world
Create yourself and you create your world. M.M.

Call me crazy, but is it possible that we literally create our world out of our own heads? There is no more perfect example of this than when we are feeling frustrated or nervous and then we suddenly trip over or hurt ourselves. Just as when we are feeling happy, we may see beauty in something we have never noticed before. Our inner feeling is mirrored in the outer circumstance. For instance, when I'm feeling good about myself and life, good things happen. When I'm not, things don't go so well. The more I have learnt this the easier it is to accept and the happier I am overall.

It means that when I'm having one of those days when everything seems to go wrong, I know that I can turn it around simply by changing my attitude. I have learnt that an annoying day or one filled with anger only farther leads me to healing, to clearing that energy, so it ultimately leads me to good. It is liberating to understand and break away from the beliefs I have learnt in life that I no longer have any need for. I accept that who I am is made up of everything that came before. To be in this moment *now* is to transcend both past and future; but we still have to deal with how we feel. It is important to remember that our memories can tie us to pain that we do not want in our present.

Here is just one example: Say I lost a rabbit as a child and it hurt me deeply. Later on in life when I hear mention of a rabbit, or see one, I may connect with this original memory and feeling of loss. Then one day I may be out with friends and hearing talk of a rabbit in the background, I may feel sad for a reason I don't even remember. Equally, if we hear a message that connects us to a positive memory we may find it serendipitous, but many may not recognise these messages if already suffering from trauma.

People can be continually hurt by their past memories. We can order our lives in such a way as to protect ourselves from the experiences or things that we perceive as causing us pain. (Remember, the greatest protector is self-love.) However, if we are not aware of what trauma or memory is plaguing us, we will probably repeat the situation, by recreating the same circumstances in our present. This is why we must be consciously aware of all our memories, and our memories of our memories. New information comes in but we may just see it in the same old way. People that feel frustrated are generally frustrating themselves with their own attitudes, usually developed through constant judgment of others and of themselves. We may continue to tell the same story, until the story itself can trap us. Some people who have suffered may find that even when things come good they are still in the same place emotionally. Because until we learn to look within and understand *why* we are the way we are, and to embrace *all* that we are, it is very hard to overcome or change the patterns that brought us to this present moment.

That being said, we all have the power to change our patterns. It can be as simple as affirming to ourselves over and over again: "I am willing to change."[129] And when wanting to let go of a negative pattern, habit or

---

[129] Hay, p. 43.

behaviour, say: "I am willing to release the need for…"[130]

Being consciously aware of the pattern is the first step to being able to break it. Because it is a choice and you can choose to change at any time you want, in any way you want. All you have to do is to give up the beliefs that are stopping you from moving forward.

Remember that the mind is a powerful thing which we tend to give the most control to, even though it is our spirit, our heart, our true essence, which ultimately guides and informs the mind.

> Do not think your mind is in control. *You* are in control of your mind. *You* use your mind. You *can* stop thinking those old thoughts. When your old thinking tries to come back and say, "It's so hard to change," take mental control. Say to your mind, "I now choose to believe it is becoming easier for me to make changes." You may have to have this conversation with your mind several times for it to acknowledge that you are in control and that what you say goes.[131]

Yet until one understands the power of one's own wisdom and is able to harness it, it can be difficult to dissolve the patterns that have manifested thus far. For example, a person that has been neglected in early life, no matter how loving people may be to them now, may always be suspicious of anything good happening, or anyone 'actually' caring. They either attract uncaring people or see only what's uncaring in people. Until they

---

[130] Hay, p. 58.
[131] Hay, p. 66.

believe within themselves that they are worthy of love, and that other people want to give love without ulterior motives, they will probably push people away. If those people then leave their life, it only farther confirms their belief that, 'people either want something from me or they don't want me at all'.

If this person then affirms, 'People love and accept me for who I am', or, "I approve of myself"[132] they are changing their outlook, or inner look, on life. An affirmation is instilled by repeating a statement over and over until it sinks in, until we believe it to be true.[133] As Hay states, for those with a negative inner dialogue: "Remember, you have been criticizing yourself for years, and it hasn't worked. Try approving of yourself and see what happens."[134] Many things can come from this. The most important one being the *difference* between what we believe and what is actually happening. For instance, continuing from the example above, after changing this inner belief through a stringent inner dialogue and then feeling more at ease with themselves, this person may begin to notice other people more. They may see that in situations where they had previously felt neglected, the person they felt neglected *by* was actually having a really bad day, or had a million things to do, and it wasn't that they didn't care; it was genuinely because they couldn't help at that time.

---

[132] Hay, p. 78.
[133] Based on Hay's advice on affirmations in *You can heal your life,* think/say positive statements in the present tense that express what you want in your life, p. 76.
[134] Hay, p. 9.

Once the person realises this, they may then recognise that in the past they had always assumed that they had been neglected, and perhaps weren't seeing life from others' point of view, as their own feelings were all-consuming.

Once they can see others' needs, reciprocal relationships can form. The next learning step is to learn to voice their own needs. If the people in their life *are* selfish, or are neglectful, the relationship isn't reciprocal. Work on it being reciprocal, or if this doesn't work, let it go.

Everyone is fulfilling everyone else's needs, just not in the way you may think. The main 'need' each of us has is to see our own inner beliefs—the way we see the world—reflected in other people and often times these beliefs are not positive! So we are creating feeling neglected, used, or hurt. Contrarily, people whose inner beliefs are those of love and peace, find this in their lives also. And this is the crucial point:

All you need to do to have love and peace in your life is to have love and peace resonating within yourself.

Think loving thoughts, be understanding with yourself. Take the time to sit quietly and let go of a barrage of thoughts. Allow mental breaks. If emotions overwhelm you, express it safely (vocalise it or hit some pillows), breathe deeply, and repeat until you feel calm.

Know you have the power to change your life completely; it is your life!

If you have allowed others to control your life, at least empower yourself from within by knowing your own

229

inner strength can do anything. If you truly believe you cannot have control over your own life, pray for the attitudes of the people around you to change, use your energy to telepathically ask for peace and love. Again, I am very sorry for those who feel that they cannot escape a negative situation right now; I pray that they'll soon be able to.

Think about this. Wonderful things cannot begin to happen for you until you believe that they can. How many times has hope gotten you out of what could have been a bad situation? How many times have you wanted something and then got it? I honestly believe that until I feel worthy of receiving, I won't actually receive. Because if I really feel I don't deserve something good I won't notice it even when it knocks at my front door. Until I can accept it I can't actually get it. I do not believe this applies to people who have absolutely no control over others. You couldn't ask a starving child to manifest food when there physically is none (although perhaps it's possible that prayer has helped some bring food to the table). But to teach someone with low self-esteem how to accept love for instance, this would require them to believe within themselves that this is possible. To feel worthy of receiving we may have to change some of our inner beliefs. If I still held some of the fundamental beliefs I had over five years ago, I would never have been able to write this book. I was struggling with life and I couldn't see beyond the struggle. But when I first had a notion that healing was important and focused on this more, amazing things happened. I finally found wonderful people to live with (in a share house); I unexpectedly received a $5000 grant from university; I won $3000 worth of prizes on a game show; I got in free to a huge rock concert; and I embarked on the first genuinely loving relationship of my life.[135] Please understand I was a person who had never attained these amounts of money previously or been self-aware enough to enjoy healthy relationships. I have had incredible experiences like this all through my life, but looking back on it, I believe I created them all simply by believing that such things could happen. When you open your heart to the possibilities, the Universe answers the call.

Yes, life can be crazy and hectic in our cities. There is way too much information (or non-information) blaring out in all manner of colour and light, that is why we must stop ourselves, every day, just stop and ask:

'Does this feel right for me?'

Listen to the inner feeling. It will tell you *exactly what you need to know,* and *exactly what you need to do,* to have a better life, or to be 'in' (being) this current moment. If you feel you cannot communicate with yourself or your intuition/instincts at this point, ask yourself about that. Once you find the reasons you are detached from your own feelings, you can then explore this. If you listen to your own inner wisdom, you will find what you seek.

I believe that every footstep, every blink, every thought, *everything* we do creates our Universe. Why? Because, how many footsteps I take to get somewhere is the

---

[135] A key factor in creating these circumstances for myself was simply repeating the "I approve of myself" affirmation from Louise L Hay's *You can heal your life* constantly for weeks; another was being introduced to Reiki.

difference between bumping into a long lost relative or not (and I have experienced this on more than one occasion). How many times I blink is the difference between seeing a shooting star or not, which is the difference between me wishing for, and giving attention to, a wish or a dream or not. Every thought I have had brings me to my current understanding. Whatever stage of the thought development is also the stage where I am ready to understand and accept new information. The more I understand, the more I understand. Humans have the ability to grow, to learn and to evolve. So here's what has to happen, according to me:

Out with the old; in with the new!!

Old beliefs must be given up; new ideas must be embraced. We may be scared of change, but is our current inhumaneness or earth-destruction how we want to live? We must understand *only we have the power to change it!! We,* meaning *every single human being that is able. For those who are oppressed must be freed by the free!!* If you are not oppressed, then you have the power to change the world. The oppressed are so busy just trying to survive; in many cases they can't rise up because they will *literally* be chopped down. We must demand that our governments act humanely! If we have armies, we must use those armies to defend the helpless, not attack the helpless or defend ourselves from 'terrorism' when by attacking without valid cause; we are in fact, asking for.

How would we demand these things? One way is through entire people networking, whereby we all communicate via the Internet, via everyone we meet, and then come up with a decent plan, even something as

232

radical as 'no one goes to work[136] or purchases from any big business until an agreement is formed between the government and the people of Australia that the military will only serve to protect and defend those being slaughtered right now. They will be the Army that Defends Human Rights. They will know the difference between the oppressors and the oppressed. (This essentially means they would defend Iraq against America, restore water and electricity—which is still not functional in most of both Iraq and Afghanistan.) Countries of the world will unite against those occupations led by the Coalition, as well as in all oppressive regimes, but not without ensuring that many other peace-keeping forces and aid agencies are put in place to assist and support the people in restoring order'.

We have an unspeakable amount to make up for.

This is how you create your Universe. You realise that by creating it you have complete control over what you do. You can maintain a calm emotional state if you choose to, no matter what the external situation is, unless you require it otherwise. You can nurture your own inner compassion and peace no matter what others say or do. Accept everything that you are in this

---

[136] For those that feel if a plan like this is ever implemented by the people at large that: 'I can't lose my job, etc.' Yes, I understand. However, if we all hold onto that attitude and refuse to make any sort of protest (particularly one that would effect change in large corporations and government policy) the people in charge will just continue to pollute our world (and abuse our fellow humans), radically damaging the possibility of a good future. Is it worth taking a risk today to create a better tomorrow? Isn't it worth the risk to make sure there are many more tomorrows?

moment and know that *you* know yourself entirely, even if you aren't perceiving your whole self in this moment. I believe that we already know everything, because every living cell in this entire Universe is connected; all we have to do is tune in.

The only things we do not know is that which we cannot yet perceive.

But we can all choose to develop our perception.

If you seek knowledge, if you seek to know yourself and the world around you, you will never stop growing or changing. Life is ever changing. Staying the same is like a tree that never sways in the wind. Like a wave that never breaks. All of life is changing and *we are life.* Of course it is the same with human beings. Our bodies are rebuilding cells and regenerating themselves even as you read!! *This is the miracle of life.* It is only the self-imposed limitations that have blinded us to the fact that we also have these incredible minds, just waiting to be filled with great ideas and thoughts, but we must willingly seek them.

Will is an inner feeling that gives us the drive to do what's required. It is important that our will and intention come from a loving place, where we are not trying to force the outside into submission, but rather allowing ourselves to flow with the inner self. That is true power.

Chapter 24 – The healing of the Human race and Planet Earth

"To the East to the West, to the North and South, to the East to the West
One love people never gonna stop"[137]

If you truly want peace no matter what else you believe, and whatever you may call God, pray for the healing of human kind and of this earth. Enact your beliefs with every thing you do and every word you say. Honour yourself and everyone around you.

I believe that ideally God would be called the Universe, or All Life or the Great Nebulae.[138] The idea of God for me personally has always represented a way to *thank life for life;* a way to pray to something outside of myself in times of need; a way to feel connected from within to a greater source; a way to recognise that we are not only physical beings, but spiritual ones. I have never cared for religion but I care very much about life and existence. Many people all over the world hold varying beliefs but do you know that we are all made up of the same cells, the same molecules? *We each have a human heart that beats and has the ability to suffer human pain.* We are all connected in this truth. We are made up of the same stuff as the star that lived and died to create the Great Nebulae from which our solar system was born. We carry the DNA of life in this Universe.

---

[137] Michael Franti & Spearhead, *East to the West,* 2006.

[138] These are groups of gas and dust clouds in our Universe that are currently spitting out new stars and creating new worlds even as we speak!! I strongly recommend you google or wikipedia search (or just go to the NASA website) to view the incredible images of these life creating nebulae.

And what we all have inside our heads is an *idea* of God (if we have any at all), and it is humans alone who say there is such a thing. This idea of God has been used to justify terrible human atrocities and violations in many religions. So we must ask ourselves: What has organised religion brought us?

> You say you're a Christian cause God made you and you say you're a Muslim cause God made you, you say you're a Hindu and the next man a Jew, then we all kill each other cause God told us to? Nah[139]

The Romans fed the Christians to the lions, during the first 4 centuries AD, until they themselves converted to Christianity in the 4th century. This new Church then went on to indoctrinate the rest of the world with their beliefs, committing countless human atrocities along the way. The fundamentalist Christians and Islamists are still enemies today, but please remember it was the Christians that, over centuries, attempted to destroy and convert Muslims across the globe, then began proclaiming Islamic knowledge as their own. There are many other wars in the world fuelled by fanatical beliefs. There are also some religions—Tibetan Buddhism being one—that practice peaceful beliefs that would never hurt anyone. Yet for the dominant organised religions of the world, peace still seems elusive.

Neale Donald Walsch, author of *The new revelations,* (his seventh book in the *Conversations with God* series) writes of his dialogue with his perception of God. In this following passage 'God' says:

---

[139] Michael Franti & Spearhead, *Hello Bonjour,* 2006.

Organized religion has been around for thousands of years. It has touched individual lives, but in your collective society it has changed little. As a group you are still dealing with the same problems that confronted you at the beginning. The problems of greed, envy, anger; righteousness, inequality, violence, and war.

…

It was hoped that religion would bring your world a greater sense of joy and freedom, but in too many cases it has not done so. In fact, few institutions have done more to bind and shackle and restrict the human spirit, presenting long lists of what one must and must not do … wear … eat … think … enjoy.[140]

My beliefs have never resonated with any organised religion as I cannot see how something as wildly beautiful and exquisite as existence itself, could ever be partitioned.

"Love is too big for just one nation and God is too big for just one religion"[141]

Cannot human beings see that they are barely even glimpsing upon the magnificence of this Universe? The magnificence which they could call God?

If what we call God is anything, it is everything, the manifestation of life itself, which means it is us also.

"God and life are the same thing."[142]

---

[140] ND Walsch, *The new revelations,* Atria/Simon and Shuster Inc., New York, 2002, p. 61.

[141] Michael Franti & Spearhead, *East to the West,* 2006.

[142] Walsch, p. 27.

To truly heal the human race we need a global belief in humanity, we need God to be seen as every living cell in this Universe, existing across all cultures and beliefs, to end all disputes. Even those who want to practise their individual faith can still join the global community and accept people's right to choose their beliefs, as long as those beliefs do not harm others. The threads of all the world's religions carry messages of peace, yet in their separation from each other they have not created this. So across all existing faiths we need *humanity to be the new religion!*[143] (The beauty is we don't even need to call it religion; we can simply call it *Global Law*.) We need beliefs that unite us all with the fundamental truth that *we can never be separate, and never have been.* A belief that accepts that we are ALL human beings, made up of the same stuff as every other being, every other atom, everything. We need to fight for it, demonstrate it, and communicate it everywhere at all times, just by being just humans. Every time we care about anyone's rights, whether it be a friend's or a stranger on the street (or ourselves!) we are demonstrating the highest degree of the humanity we are capable of. This humanity must reside in our hearts and minds. We must communicate telepathically through meditation and prayer, and even through thoughts alone. Collectively, we can do great things, but as individuals, we have power over every second, and it is a choice whether we love or resent,

---

[143] The documentary *Soldiers of Peace* (2008) shows wonderful examples of how people are learning to practice peace across all faiths; even with those religious practitioners that people once considered their enemies. I highly recommend this film for all those interested in how to create peace across different cultures and within one's individual powers.

forgive or hate, heal or hurt. Think about this: Which one will bring you closer to the peace we all seek? Which one will not?

And we need voters; lots and lots of voters. We may not *like* the system but we can *change* the system. We may not like the contenders, so we won't vote for any of them, until new ones are sought. We must all care we must all care we must all care we must all care we must all care we must all care we must all care we must all care we must all care we must all care we must all care we must all care we must all care we must all care we must all care we must all care we must all care we must all care we must all care we must all care ad infinitum.

We must all care and be informed and not give an inch when it comes to others causing human suffering. It's that simple.

For society to get healthier and more humane right now, we need all the people we can to monitor governments (our own and those across the world) and their actions and protest in every way possible; send floods of emails and mail, write songs, get heard, and see just how many of us there really are. We can start our own groups online and build the Collective. We can communicate at mass levels and we can be heard. We can be resourceful (just look at the work of the Get-Up campaign). We can start growing our own veggies if we have room for a garden; we can recycle our water and learn to be self-sufficient. We can buy a water tank and filtration system, and buy our staples cheaply at markets. When we take those dollars that fill the pockets of the filthy we begin to show just how much our own individual power can cost. Every person counts!

We must stop indulging in our selfish lifestyle at the expense of millions of our fellow human beings on Planet Earth. Consider this: If we were all educated and informed about government policy and taught the democratic ways of holding governments accountable, we would know how to force those governments to adhere to international laws, to the laws that uphold human rights.

Sanity needs to be a fundamental factor in society; the simple art of truth seeking being so important in this modern world filled with such a huge amount of information, some of it convoluted. Intelligence, ideas and dreams must be pursued freely and encouraged and nurtured; as we all have something important to offer; our own special niche.[144] People need to be raised with love and respect so that they can then demonstrate this in their own lives.

Education must teach the functions of the brain, heart, and mind and how this relates to one's everyday life. It should be paid for only by those who can afford it and free for those who can't. (Remember, those who implemented fees for universities in Australia are the same people who got their degrees for free; a generation or so ago *there was no $20 000 debt!*) Our young will learn about the nature of our political systems. They will

---

[144] The rationalists may argue that 'we need all kinds of workers for society to function and it may not be someone's dream to work in a chicken farm'. Well here's one solution: how about, we convert to vegetarianism and take more responsibility for making our own food, say, with each household given the resources to grow simple grain and vegetables and those who are able to, fund it themselves. Problem solved.

learn about living in a society that strives for social justice in all ways. They will learn how to handle their emotions and how to deal with their prejudices. Teachers will not act solely as authority figures, but of mediums of knowledge and wisdom, recognising each individual's own abilities and capabilities.

Young people must be given a fundamental right to express their views and be heard; perhaps even allowed some form of mini-vote. At the very least they should be informed and recognised for what they think.

The Australian people as a whole must reconcile with its Indigenous race. This means talking *with* and working out solutions that recognise what these people actually want and need to live life with dignity. Obviously reconciliation does not mean mapping out what we (the government) want for them (the Indigenous). It means that we come together as a country and apologise for our incredibly destructive treatment of them. There must be a national apology, and we will work with the Indigenous to create a better and more loving and tolerant society for *all* Australians.

For all people to live fairly, the richest must be taxed the heaviest, and the poor not taxed at all. But where will the taxes go? Where they should go: into welfare, education, and hospitals. Money must be distributed justly. The government will give up its life of luxury cars and homes, and the money left will go directly into supporting the homeless, those with disabilities, and rehabilitating those with drug addictions. The taxing of the rich will directly help to alleviate the misery of the poor. We need humble leaders that will not bathe in taxpayers' money.

241

Humans must give up their addictions to materialism and focus their energies on healing themselves and the planet. There is no point having a $50 000 Porsche, if it means your lineage aint got no planet to drive it in. We must give up our addictions to perpetual emotional states. We must rise above our differences. People need to communicate honestly, and value honesty. The government will ultimately reflect the society, and therefore make valuable contributions to human rights here and everywhere. People have created civilized living, and have since then helped to destroy it. It is time for our civilizations to be based on knowledge and potential, rather than fear, competition and greed.

These are my visions for a future that has hope.

And now, as we come to the end of this book—although the end is only the beginning—I want to leave you with these thoughts:

Apparently those smart scientists have figured out that most stars—of which our sun is only *one*—exist for about 10 billion years. Our sun is currently 4.6 odd billion years old, roughly halfway through its lifecycle. Out of all the other worlds that could possibly exist, considering the trillions plus stars there are, what do we want to be the legacy of this world? The legacy of the human race? Is it possible that it is our ultimate quest to create a legacy that is one of peace? That even with the history of violence, and maybe because of it, human beings all over the world, and all through human history, have continued to hope and pray that peace will ultimately be the outcome? Why are our favourite stories always the ones of humans overcoming great odds to reach a goal or to get through an illness? It's because each of these stories reminds us of the lesson of appreciation and inspires in us utter admiration for the power of the human spirit. It reminds us that anything is possible as long as we believe it *is* possible. And if we all believe in peace (which we all desire for ourselves) what if it is within us to overcome these great obstacles in the way of peace? And up to all of us to create it?

There are over 6 billion people on this planet who need peace, and a whole world that needs saving.

Anodea Judith writes in *Wheels of life: a user's guide to the chakra system,* that the human race since its inception has been evolving through the seven chakras[145] but because we have cut ourselves off from our roots (first chakra—element Earth), and our sexuality and emotions (second chakra—element Water), as well as using our will over others, or giving away our own personal power (third chakra—element Fire) we are struggling to acknowledge that we are currently journeying through the fourth chakra (element Air).[146]

> The dawning of the Age of Aquarius, a fixed air sign, marks the true arrival of the Age of the Heart Chakra, with an emphasis on humanitarianism, compassion, self-reflection, integration and healing. It is the peace that emerges within and without when the essential balance has been achieved.[147]

---

[145] A chakra is a word used to describe the energy fields of the body.
[146] A Judith, *Wheels of life: A user's guide to the chakra system,* Llewellyn publications, USA, 1999, p. 380.
[147] Judith, p. 396.

Everything every individual does on this planet, affects positively or negatively the future that is to come.

> *What do you want for 50 years time? Everything that you do shapes its truth, 'cause if the meaning of life, is the human spirit that never dies, let it guide you, let it guide you, let it guide you to fight for life, for the sacredness of human life ... for the sacredness of all life*[148]

We can let the humans in power destroy and control us all, or we can all, choose to fight for peace.

> *The passion in our souls, more powerful than any weapon*
> *But if we want it to be known, we've got to show it this very second*
> *I said the passion in our souls, more powerful than any manmade weapon but if we want the madmen who run this world to be overthrown, we've got to show ourselves this very second*[149]

The time ... to act ... is NOW!

I love you all.

The End.

---

[148] Jess Hieser, *Meaning of life,* unreleased music single, Jess Hieser, 2007.

[149] Jess Hieser, *Propaganda,* unreleased music single, Jess Hieser, 2004.

END NOTES

October 28th 2008

In the time taken writing this book, Israel has destroyed much of Lebanon; the U.S. military has crossed borders into Pakistan; Africans continue to suffer unimaginably; the Palestinians are even more oppressed; peace-loving Tibetans are being beaten to death; and many over the world are living in intolerable conditions. All this is virtually ignored—or seen once on the news and then forgotten—by the Australian public, but in all these cases *it is real human beings who are being affected!*

Most of the lies about the premise for going to war with Iraq have been made public. The U.S. administration has violated many international laws, yet is still functioning as a war machine even though the Bush II government is falling apart at the seams. As I add my final notes, the 2008 U.S. presidential election is less than a week away. I pray that American voters elect the Democrats and ultimately work towards a system where both sides up for election are not only centre-right, but include parties centre-left. The belief that a socially inclusive form of government is in some way negative to society is only held by those who have a lot to gain from capitalism, such as control of all the profits. Why would any human be against something that could benefit all humans? Barrack Obama, for any rhetoric of him being a Socialist, is in fact reasonably conservative, yet still the changes he represents for the U.S. people (and hopefully the greater world) could be astronomical; at the very least a renewed interest in voting and being politically engaged holds U.S. citizens in good stead to better charter the course of their own destiny. John

McCain may be a half decent Republican (if that's possible), due to his experience with war, but he is still a Republican, whose running mate has violated her own state's ethics laws. Yet it seems even when the U.S. government changes its leader, it doesn't necessarily change its policies, so the bigger picture is the complete de-structuring and re-structuring of how the U.S. (and other like-minded nations) conducts its governments. If the U.S. could become a truly just country of the world, by dismantling its military campaigns of dominance in many nations, and begin to work on the healing of all affected regions, the possibility of World Peace becomes much less of a pipe dream, and closer to being a reality.

Keep in mind that when a moderate government takes position from one that was right to far-right wing, there is a great deal of damage to repair, not to mention the time it takes to implement better policies. This is the case with the change-over governments of Kennet-Bracks (Victoria 1999), Howard-Rudd (Australia 2007), and soon to be Bush-Obama. It takes more than a few years to repair broken down health, education and welfare systems; in these cases patience is needed but people must still work to keep the new governments accountable, learning the lessons of the past, whilst continuing to move forward towards more solidarity and greater humanity. The time for great change is here, and now more than ever we need to keep the momentum going; not ever allowing ourselves to fall back into the complacency that led to the extremism of the Coalition, whilst continuing to fight fiercely for the rights of people and the environment the world over. By electing humane governments in our own countries we put ourselves in a position where *we can begin to effect positive change in all these situations.* If enough countries of the world were bound by peace, it is possible that eventually we could have peace in all countries.

The most important thing we need to do is to not ever give up hope in our fight for human rights for All, and most especially, to never give up on ourselves and our own personal goals, as it is our own well-being that gives us the strength to fight for others.

Our world is being deeply divided in many countries and in many ways. The added issues arising from the global economic crisis, and global warming, is even more reason for us to solve these problems together. We must unite the human race through compassion for *all* beings. This begins with one word, one action, one person, one city, one state, one country; and never ceasing until we have One World.

Thanks to all those who have supported the writing of this book. You know who you are. And to all of you: *thanks for listening.*

See you next in *The Awakening.* M.M.

REFERENCES

Books:

Ardagh, Arjuna Nick, *Relaxing into Clear Seeing,* SelfXpress, California, 1998.

Chomsky, Noam, *Hegemony or survival,* Allen & Unwin, Australia & New Zealand, 2003. Published by arrangement with Harold Holt and company, LLC, USA, 2003.

Hay, Louise L, *You can heal your life,* Hayhouse Inc., USA, 1999.

Judith, Anodea, *Wheels of life: a user's guide to the chakra system,* Llewellyn publications, USA, 1999.

Kalinkova, Ivarna, *The Wisdom Well,* Quarto Publishing, London, Quarto Inc., 2003.

Lidell, Lucy, with Narayani and Giris Rabinovitch, *The book of Yoga,* Edbury Press/Gaia Books Limited, Great Britain, 1983.

Moore, Michael, *Stupid White Men,* Regan Books/HarperCollins Publishers Inc., United States, 2001.

Orwell, George, *1984,* Penguin Books, England, 1954. First published 1949.

Orwell, George, *Homage to Catalonia,* Penguin Books, England, 1962. First published 1938.

Peck, Scott, *The Road Less Travelled,* Simon and Shuster, United States, 1978.

Plato, *The Republic,* Penguin Group, England, 1955.

Rashid, Ahmed, *Taliban,* Pan McMillan Ltd, London, 2001.

The Dalai Lama, HH, *The little book of Buddhism,* Rider/Random House, London, 2000.

The Dalai Lama, HH, *The little book of Wisdom,* Rider/Random House, London, 2000.

248

Tolstoy, Leo, *War and Peace,* Pan Books Ltd, London, 1972. First published 1904.

Walsch, Neale Donald, *The new revelations,* Atria/Simon and Shuster Inc., New York, 2002.

Documentaries:

Achbar, Mark, Bakan, Joel, Abbott, Jennifer, *The Corporation,* Big Picture Media Corporation MMIII, USA, 2004.

Gardner, Robert, *Islam: Empire of Faith,* Gardner films Inc./PBS, USA, 2000.

Greenwald, Robert, *Uncovered: the whole truth about the Iraq War,* Caroline Productions Inc., USA, 2004.

Moore, Michael *Fahrenheit 9/11,* Hopscotch entertainment Pty, Ltd, Westside productions LLC, USA, 2004.

Schechter, Danny, *Weapons of Mass Deception,* WMD GlobalVision LP, USA, 2004.

Vicente, Mark, Arntz, William, Chasse, Betsy, *What the bleep do we know?* MMIV Lord of the Wind Films, LLC, USA, 2004.

Television programs:

Australian Broadcasting Corporation, *Catalyst,* Australia, Aired 9 August 2007.

Australian Broadcasting Corporation, *Compass: Islam on Parade,* Australia, Aired 16 October 2005.

Australian Broadcasting Corporation, *We of little voice,* Australia, Aired 18 June 2007.

Special Broadcasting Service, *Newshour,* (from PBS, U.S.), Australia, Aired 1 August 2007.

Journals and Newspapers:

Chandrasekaran, Rajiv, 'U.S. only spent 2% of its aid package', *The Age,* 5 July 2004.
Labor Review, Victorian Labor College, No. 41, Autumn, 2005.
Masud, Edward 'War on terror or a war on Islam?', *New Dawn Magazine,* No. 88, Jan/Feb 2005.
Waleed, Aly, 'How many innocent Iraqis is too many?' *The Age,* 9 November 2004.

Internet:

www.politicalhumor.about.com/od/bushquotes/Bushisms Accessed on February 12th 2006.
http://en.wikipedia.org/wiki/Call_of_Duty_4_Modern_ Warfare
Sales at May 2009. Accessed on July 19th 2009.
**Please note this is the only reference made in the 2009 edit (all other references to October 2008).

Music:

Jess Hieser, *Change from within,* unreleased music single, Australia, © 2007.
Jess Hieser, *Meaning of life,* unreleased music single, Australia, © 2007.
Jess Hieser, *Propaganda,* unreleased music single, Australia, © 2004.
Michael Franti and Spearhead, *Everyone Deserves Music,* Album, Michael Franti, Boo Boo Wax, USA, © 2003.
Michael Franti and Spearhead, *Yell Fire!* Album, Michael Franti, Boo Boo Wax, USA, © 2006.
The Living End, *White Noise,* Album, Chris Cheney, Dew Process, Australia, © 2008.

RESOURCES

<u>Books</u>

Daniele Archibugi: *The Global Commonwealth of Citizens*
David Held & Anthony McGrew: *Globalization/Anti-globalization*
Larry Diamond: *The Spirit of Democracy*
George Orwell: *1984*
Noam Chomsky: *Hegemony or survival*
Noam Chomsky: *World orders, old and new*
David Rose: *Guantanamo: America's war on human rights*
Ahmed Rashid: *Taliban*
S. H. Hooke: *Middle Eastern mythology*
Louise L Hay: *You can heal your life*
Sanaya Roman: *Spiritual Growth: Being your Higher Self*
Scott Peck: *The road less traveled*
Ramacha Raka: *Psychic healing*
Annie Bessant: *The Ancient Wisdom*
The Universal Declaration of Human Rights

<u>Documentaries/Films/TV</u>

All Michael Moore documentaries: *Bowling for Columbine, Fahrenheit 9/11, Roger and Me, Sicko, the Awful Truth, etc.*
All Robert Greenwald documentaries (see links below).
Michael Franti: *I am not alone*
Danny Schechter: *Weapons of Mass Deception*
Morgan Spurlock: *Super Size Me*
Noam Chomsky: *Manufacturing consent*
Pat McNamara: *The Fog of War*
Rabbit Proof Fence

251

The Corporation
What The Bleep Do We Know/Down the Rabbit Hole
SBS: *World news, Dateline, Foreign correspondent, Living Black, etc.*
ABC: *7.30 report, Big Ideas, Parliament, National press club, etc.*
Channel 31: *Conversations with Robyn, Words of peace, Slow TV, etc.*

Authors/People/Artists

Michael Franti, Michael Moore, Ahmed Rashid, Pat Dodson, Xavier Rudd, Ruby Hunter, Archie Roach, Eddie Vedder, Bono, Louise L Hay, Cathy Freeman, Bob Dylan, Chomsky, Bob Brown, David Suzuki, Peter Singer, All Who Care.

Radio

3CR Community Radio
ABC Radio National
PBS Radio

Websites

America and War:

www.michaelmoore.com
www.pbs.org/newshour (Independent American news channel)
www.costofwar.com
www.americanprogress.org
www.robertgreenwald.org
www.moveon.org
www.truthuncovered.com.au
www.iraqforsale.org

www.outfoxed.org
www.unprecedented.org
www.wmdthefilm.com

Indigenous Australia:

www.dreamtime.net.au
www.apo.org.au (Australian Policy Online)
www.scu.edu.au (Gnibi College of Indigenous Australians)
http://Indigenousaustralia.frogandtoad.com.au
www.idb.org (Indigenous people of Australia)
www.reconcile.org.au
www.womenforwik.org
www.seaofhands.org.au (Australians for Native Title and Reconciliation)
www.nit.com.au (National Indigenous Times)
www.3knd.org.au (Indigenous radio station)
www.closethegap.org.au

Humanitarian:

www.asrc.org.au (Asylum Seeker Resource Centre)
www.orphfund.org
www.redcross.org
www.greenpeace.org.au
www.hrw.org (Human Rights Watch)
www.hsi.org (Humane Society International)
www.unicef.org.au (UN International Children's Emergency Fund)
www.makepovertyhistory.org
www.closeguantanamo.org
www.aidwatch.org.au
www.amnesty.org.au
www.action.amnesty.org.au

253

www.msf.org.au (Medecins Sans Frontieres)
www.hraff.org.au (Human Rights Arts and Film festival)
www.caresuatralia.org.au
www.tamera.org
www.unity4sisters.org
www.awsa.org.au (Australian Western Sahara Association)

Environment:

www.foei.org (Friends Of the Earth International)
www.foe.org.au (Friends Of the Earth Australia)
www.acfonline.org.au (Australian Conservation Foundation)
www.beyondzeroemissions.org
www.votenuclearfree.net
www.nukefreeaus.org
www.no-waste.org
www.beyondnuclearinitiative.wordpress.com
www.anvilhill.org.au
www.risingtide.org.au
www.wwf.org (World Wildlife fund)
www.savethewhales.org
www.wilderness.org.au
www.asen.org.au (Australian Student Environment Network)
www.antinuclear.net
www.anawa.org.au (Anti-Nuclear Alliance of Western Australia)
www.ecoclubs.com.au
www.earthtribe.com.au
www.coolmelbourne.org
www.reefcheckaustralia.org
www.thingreenline.org
www.fauna-flora.org.au
www.live.org.au (Locals into Victoria's environment)

www.envirolink.org
www.ceres.org.au
(Centre for Education and Research in Environmental Strategies)

Healing:

www.yogaindailylife.org.au Yoga
www.reikiaustralia.com.au Reiki
www.taichiaustralia.com.au Tai Chi

You can find practitioners and classes in your area through these sites, or check what's available in your city or town.

Other Knowledge/Interest:

www.sbs.com.au
www.abc.net.au
www.theage.com.au
www.pbsfm.org.au
www.c31.org.au (Channel 31 – c31)
www.wordsofpeace.org.au (c31)
www.conversationswithrobyn.com (c31)
www.vicfairtrade.org.au
www.ethical.org.au
www.thecorporation.com
www.whatthebleep.com
www.controlroommovie.com
http://english.aljazeera.net/english
www.en.wikipedia.org
www.mediachannel.org (link to the book *Weapons of Mass Deception*)
www.rocktheboat.com
www.hayhouse.com

www.hayhouseradio.com
www.ableaustralia.org.au
www.melbournesocialforum.org

Political-Global:

www.worldbank.org
www.forbes.com
www.tradewatchoz.org (Global trade watch)
www.globalpolicy.org
www.constitution.org
www.islamic-world.net
www.opendemocracy.net
www.whitehouse.gov
http://europa.eu (European Union)
www.politicalcompass.org (Includes a test to assess political leanings)
www.cia.gov (Central Intelligence Agency)
www.un.org (United Nations)

Political-Local:

www.getup.org.au
www.themonthly.com.au (Slow TV)
www.zeitgeistaustralia.org
www.citizensparliment.org.au

Musicians:

Michael Franti and Spearhead:
www.spearheadvibrations.com.au
www.powertothepeaceful.org (Check out the list under 'Social Justice'.)
www.iamnotalone.com
www.whatibe.org

Other (Australia):

www.katienoonan.com
www.thelivingend.com
www.ashgrunwald.com
www.archieroach.com.au
www.myspace.com/xavierrudd
www.johnbutlertrio.com
www.pearljam.com (U.S.)

Local musicians (Melbourne, VIC):

www.facebook.com/jesshieser
www.facebook.com/songwriterscollective
www.myspace.com/thejayden
 www.myspace.com/elftranzporter

To check out the Greens, go to:

www.greens.org.au

To write to the Australian Prime Minister go to:

www.pm.gov.au

To write to the American president, go to:

comments@whitehouse.gov

To write to me via email go to:

awakenworld@hotmail.com
www.facebook.com/MarthaMansfieldBooks

PLEASE NOTE: These are some of the links that have helped me on my journey. There is always more that I need to know, that I need to grow. I encourage you to explore any avenues that you feel drawn to. You can request extra copies of this book via Balboa press.

IDEAS AND SOLUTIONS
Complete.

PART ONE – Humanity

Chapter 1 – Wake Up World

- Vote Howard out.
- Do not judge what you do not understand. Develop your understanding.
- Fight for human rights in every way you can; talk to people!
- Watch documentaries, read books, seek the truth for yourself; mine is only one view.
- Whatever your opinion of Michael Moore, he does reveal the links between oil in the Middle East and the U.S. administration well in *Fahrenheit 9/11*.
- Analyse the polls; ask about second preference votes and where they go. Do not vote Family First, they are a fundamentalist Christian group which ultimately represses freedom. Labour have been supporting many of Howard's policies (and are closer to centre-right due to Howard's extremism), so unless they improve, the only decent option is the Greens. A Greens government would at least show the world we are committed to Peace and the Planet, rather than war and money. However, we need Labour in government until there are enough Green seats for the majority parties to be Labour and the Greens.
- Join any human rights activist groups that you can.

259

- The only reason the Howard government has managed to produce low unemployment figures is because Howard has created new laws forcing welfare recipients to work (for nix or as little as $30 a fortnight) to retain their welfare payment. Even 1 hour of unpaid work counts as employment which is why the 'work for the dole' scheme has been so effective in raising employment figures. Similarly our economy is only 'booming' because the rich are making a lot of money (and of course there are all those mining exports to China) while the poor are getting ripped off even more.
- Just remember, you have been given this incredible gift of life, and it can never be justified that we have this at the expense of those who are being deprived of their gift of life. To truly appreciate what we have, we need to start working on this incredible inequality *now*.

Chapter 2 – Prejudice

- Seek information on the history of Islam. Look at the parallels between the cities Islam created, and our own democracy.
- All we have to do to turn the tides in favour of human rights is to communicate it emphatically to all people, including those in power. You can email and write letters to any member of the government, demanding that justice be sought for any issue you feel is valuable. How easy is it to write an email?
- If you are passionate enough about social justice issues, become an independent, or join the Greens.

- Apologise on behalf of our country to our Indigenous and our Muslim residents whenever you get the opportunity.
- It is important to remember that America and Australia are two of the youngest countries in the world. Both slaughtered the Indigenous populations to claim the land. Both have an extensive history of conquering and of war (descending from England) and both have created (at least for the majority of their citizens) an empty wasteful culture, unlike the nations we are attacking now which have thousands of years of history, and rich complex cultures. We must expand our knowledge on these matters.
- There are many people who have fled from war in Australia right here, right now. A $5-10 a month donation, or some of that tinned food in your cupboard, could be feeding many families in urgent need. You can donate to the Asylum Seeker Resource Centre.
- I strongly encourage you to join, or at least check out, the Get-Up campaign. This is a non-partisan grass-roots movement in Australia taking positive and practical action on many important issues.
- Bring awareness to other Australians about the struggles of our Indigenous people whenever possible. The Northern Territory intervention is only creating more fear; why use the military when your goal is to protect children? It is horrendous. These communities need support and funding, not soldiers. Many of these communities have been neglected for decades and beyond; what is needed is reconciliation and

a strong Indigenous voice in the Australian government.

Chapter 4 – What can you do?

- Don't ever underestimate your own personal power to change yourself and the world for the better.
- Here are some individual actions which could create positive change: use durable and absorbent biodegradable clothe bags instead of plastic for waste disposal and encourage those in your circle to do the same; reduce purchasing plastic wherever possible and email companies requesting they use more environmentally friendly packaging; if you own shares in the stock market, make sure that those companies you've invested in adhere to practices that are both humane and not destructive to the environment and encourage those you know with shares to do the same; start a chain letter which lists the details of humanitarian and environmental non-profit organisations that can be donated to (even if only $5 a month) and deliver to the houses on your street and/or your circle of friends encouraging them to forward on the information.
- Consider that ideas you have about bettering yourself and humanity may be very important information for others to consider also. Talk to those people you feel are open-minded; share your ideas with the community by writing to the local paper or newsletter. Remember all the great ideas in history started with a small seed in an individual's or group's mind.

- People have so many varying interests and it's only natural that some of us feel more strongly about certain issues whether its animal rights, the environment, famine or the treatment of those in our local aged care facility. If we truly honour that which we feel passionate about we can donate, support, volunteer, and vocalise (through meetings or sending emails) our thoughts on these matters, which is a great contribution to the whole. There are so many wonderful organisations covering a huge range of issues that are working hard to right wrongs and heal crises; the more support they have the stronger their weight in terms of influencing changes in government policy where its needed to truly solve the problem. This is why emailing governments is often just as important as making donations to organisations that are ethical in their work.

PART TWO – The ways we deny our own humanity

Chapter 5 – Lack of awareness

For those who desire it here are some basic steps on the journey to self-discovery:

- Look inward; what have you learnt about life and how does this shape your life? What morals has this developed in you? How much do you need to be right? Or what do you feel is wrong? Do you trust your instincts? Do you examine your true feelings? Do you act with compassion? Are you close with others who support you and your dreams? How can you develop your ability to love and to receive love? Be willing to get to know ... yourself.

- Be open-minded; when you hear new information, do not disregard it. Be willing to search for truth that will enrich and broaden your understanding, not diminish it. Be open to different opportunities or ideas even if they make you feel uncomfortable initially. Usually what we resist the most helps to teach us the lessons we most need to learn. Sometimes the resistance might tell us what we don't want, or don't like, which can be very self-revealing; other times it can be that something's hit a nerve, and wherever that nerve is, it's a part of us that's seeking to be healed.

- The documentary *What the bleep do we know?* offers excellent insights into how our conditioning works amidst its extensive discussions on quantum theory.

- Trust your basic truths; the greatest truth of humankind is love. I believe true loving means having compassion for all life including our own, and acting accordingly.

Chapter 6 – Guilt

- Instead of complaining (if you do); appreciate everything!

- Reach out to those you love rather than pushing them away. If you cannot trust them with your vulnerability, try to see the vulnerability in them. Perhaps they are displaying theirs in a different way to you (for example, some people respond with anger when they feel vulnerable). If neither of you are growing, at least take the time to focus on your own growth.

- Relationships *can be* tricky. We are essentially combining our own inner reality with another's but if we understand that our own conditioning colours our view, it is much easier to diagnose problems in our interactions. This does take a certain amount of maturity; the act of being able to admit one's needs or negative behaviour during arguments or tense interactions means taking full responsibility for oneself. This doesn't mean we sugarcoat it if others behave badly, as we must be firm with any person who acts disrespectfully, but in understanding the fears, beliefs, hopes or failings in our own behaviour, it's much easier to understand these behaviours in others and therefore work towards more mutually empowering relationships.

- The West is currently embracing many paths to healing. Yet there is an argument going around that this is merely more self-indulgence. Although this may be true for some, you will find that most, if not all, people that seek healing do so because they are suffering in some way. Healing is a way for people to see what that suffering is about and to heal by returning to wholeness. An important aspect to healing is to understand the truth; that we are *not* alone, *not* separate, but rather connected to *all* life. While we're on the subject though, one way to cure any self-indulgence is to play our own parts in creating peace; in our own hearts, in our own lives, in our own streets.

Chapter 7 – Distraction

- Put down your heavy burdens, even if just for a moment, take a deep breath and let it all go. Know that in this current moment just by changing your thinking or your perspective, you can change what is not working for you.
- Explore any or all methods of healing that you are drawn to.
- Take the chance to explore a dream you may not have followed. We generally create the most prosperity by doing what we are truly drawn to and what makes us truly happy.
- If you are materialistic, try encouraging Australian businesses to offer jobs to the Indigenous or homeless here rather than exploiting foreign workers.

Chapter 8 – Television

- Read George Orwell's *1984*. The implications of this book are only becoming more relevant in our current societal set-up.
- Turn off the TV! Read or muse instead.
- Write to the Free TV body and to the communications Minister if you feel there is any truth in my observations. Keep in mind that the Free TV ads began shortly after the use of sex and violence on TV in Australia increased dramatically (post the free-trade agreement). By giving people the option, some may feel they don't need to express their concerns; they believe that others will do that for them. In many cases to effect change, that 'other' person

needs to be you (me).

- During the Vietnam War, footage of the atrocities was shown on TV and many people reacted to the images. They felt that it was valuable to bear witness to the truth of those atrocities, and seeing what was actually happening gave them impetus on which to act (remember the images of children exposed to Napalm used by the U.S. and allies). I have heard people of that era say, 'We knew that society wouldn't stand for it'. Yet, just 40 years later, the same kind of images are shown on TV without penetrating the most part of society. I know this because Howard was voted back in. It is devastating that our senses are now so dulled that horrific images of people suffering through these wars that we actively support does not create a prominent backlash in our societies as it did back then; the nature of human suffering hasn't changed, only our lack of response to it.
- Our young are so exposed to, and influenced by, TV. It is essential that we encourage them to be free, compassionate and discerning thinkers.

Chapter 9 – Advertising

- Whatever your issue, I strongly recommend meditation, Yoga, Tai Chi. You need to help your body feel wonderful, once you stop hating and despising it, you will give it a chance to regain health by making it *feel good!* Very important.
- Note your facial expressions. Do you try to look a certain way to people? If so, a lot of your time may be spent thinking about how others view

you. Try to go beyond that, actually *be*ing with people, with a neutral face and relaxed demeanour.

- Please watch *Super Size Me*.[150] Allow yourself to get angry at the fast food corporations who are recklessly endangering our health without any moral or ethical considerations.

- Put all the money you put into beauty into humanity or your life's dream.

- Remember, my fellow women sisters: If we all did this (let the hair grow back, give up the make-up etc.) we would be rebelling together! We are protected in numbers. The masses accept what the masses do. We could turn this whole world around if we starved the beauty industry of finance and put that money into politics or social change. To achieve this goal all that is needed is to start a fashion trend (it would help if some celebs got on board) whereby it's 'cool' to be natural; i.e., no make-up or shaving etc. Just think of the savings. Yes, many women say, 'I do it because it makes me feel good'; I just wonder if they would say the same thing if it was considered unpopular in society to wear make-up or shave.

- An excellent relaxation technique is to mentally tell parts of your body to relax. One name for this technique is called Auto-suggestion; this example is used during the final relaxation pose of a Yoga session. (Of course you can do it anytime you want.) "I relax the toes, I relax the toes. The toes *are* relaxed. I relax the calves, I

---

[150] A documentary of one man attempting to eat nothing but Macca's (McDonalds) for 30 days.

268

relax the calves. The calves *are* relaxed."[151] Repeat for all areas of the body. It can help to physically tense and release each area before saying or thinking the above instructions.

Chapter 11 – Self-abuse

- Please trust that once you can open up to someone, once you believe that there is hope, that the will of the human spirit is mighty and can take you wherever you want to go. Believe that others can help, and they can. Just remember each human being is walking around in their own headspace, trying to overcome their own issues, whatever they may be. Be willing to see others, and to allow others to see you. Be open to healing, be open to changing; and I send love to all those suffering.

- I do believe Louise L Hay's book *You can heal your life* is an excellent do-it-yourself healing manual. If you can overcome any judgments you may have and be willing to use the tools with an open heart, its possible; you really can heal your life. Sounds corny I know, but that's a judgment. It is not necessarily healthy that many of us are cynical about the processes, avenues and even the terms of healing, whatever they are. We must release these outmoded judgments if we are to allow ourselves to accept healing, (much needed by all humans), in any of its shapes or forms.

- If you are hurting yourself or living in a negative way, sometimes simply adding some

---

[151] Lidell, p. 27.

good into your life can put you on the road to recovery. For instance, rather than a smoker or alcoholic trying to quit, they could commit to a daily walk and drinking more water. For negative thinking, one could choose to annul one self-criticism a day with a single thought 'I love and accept myself'. Sometimes adding good into a dark situation is the best way to gradually come out of it.

- One of the ultimate healing techniques is to wish no harm, and even to send love to those that have hurt you. I know some people may think this is insane, but it is one way that may help restore our power, by maintaining human decency, regardless of others' actions. I have come to appreciate those experiences that I once perceived as terrible, because everything I have experienced has made me who I am today, and I need to accept all that I am to be at peace.

Chapter 13 – Violent computer games

- If you want to do a quick check on how much influence computer games are having in your life, draw a chart of your activities and the time spent on them. You could span this over a week or five years, (just do rough estimates). For instance, how many frags have you clocked up over how much time? How much time spent watching TV? How much time spent walking, relaxing, reading, writing, reflecting, following your life's dream, etc.? Once you've done a rough chart look at how high the levels are for violent games or TV and measure against the time taken for personal growth.

- Some players say that playing violent games increases their confidence, plus they get to 'meet' people online and learn about role playing, decision making and different game techniques. I still say that good old fashioned social interaction and learning that which will be practised in the *real* world, are far healthier and more productive pursuits than that which can be gained via simulation.

- *Good Game* is amongst a new breed of TV shows that review games, including ones graphically violent. Using terms like 'war' and 'grenade' in game review is normal, when this in fact completely disrespects all those at war right now. Please Wake Up World!!

- Consider that the first-shooter game *Call of Duty 4: Modern Warfare,* has sold over 13 million copies since 2007.[152] This figure is close to the current amount of displaced refugees from Iraq, Palestine and Afghanistan combined from recent conflicts (over 15 million). On the one hand, you have the players of *Call of Duty 4: Modern Warfare,* and on the other you have real people who have fled from war. Is this not a frightening circumstance? What would happen if both these groups could be swapped for a day? Do you think those refugees would want to play a realistic war game? If you think they wouldn't, and consider why they wouldn't, ask yourself why it is that you do.

---

[152] http://en.wikipedia.org/wiki/Call_of_Duty_4_Modern_ Warfare
Sales at May 2009. Accessed on July 19th 2009.

Chapter 14 – Addictions in society

- In relation to breaking patterns, my advice is to be open-minded about changing your responses. For instance, just because you may be a person who often gets angry or impatient in traffic or when kept waiting, doesn't mean you have to continue doing so. I often used to become very frustrated when waiting in queues, until I read a book that advised sending healing light and gratitude to people. I started practising this when waiting in line and things always went well, because no matter what the external situation was, I was feeling too peaceful for it to bother me. To help the line move faster I also think thoughts such as: 'The line moves easily; I am happy to be here; I may even run into somebody or experience serendipity because of the time this takes' (and I often have!). I use the time to think about anything I need or want to, whether it's remembering or planning or daydreaming. I send love and compassion to those around me and send understanding to others' frustration. I see that we are not separate; I have merely chosen to change my response. Again, the book *You can heal your life* by Louise L Hay is highly recommended here for help with changing your thinking and making better choices.

Another example: I was once at an intimate music concert where some university students were squashing me in and talking very loudly about toilets! They started grating on my nerves; their voices were right in my ear, I didn't have enough room to move, and I was getting too hot in a crowded room. In the past I would probably have overloaded and had to leave momentarily. But then I remembered that I control my own state, so I started using the method I have described above, adapting the thoughts to the situation, for instance: 'I am calm; I release the need to be annoyed; I have plenty of room to move'. Within a few minutes of me doing this, the conversation changed. The students started talking about *An Inconvenient Truth* and the environment. One of their friends with a very loud voice left and there was more room for me to move. In my own experience, when I am willing to change myself and my thinking, the external situations respond accordingly.

Chapter 16 – Drugs and alcohol

- The irony about drugs is that the less we intake of any drug whether its pot, alcohol, or heroin, the greater its effect. We actually need very little of any drug to get 'high' if we are well-rounded and healthy people. The problem is the more we take of any of these drugs, the more we need to get the same high which is when the heavy addictions and problems start. The answer is to do *anything* healthy, whether its soaking in a spa; getting a massage; having raw fruit and veg juices; gently exercising; drinking water; sleeping enough so that its fully replenishing; having a luxuriant bath; eating great food, particularly with toxin purges like garlic and chilli; cleansing drinks and teas (like green tea). Put any self-nurturing acts such as these into the repertoire of your daily routine, ideally combined with taking less of any drug—even if only a little less—whilst continuing to insert these healthy acts and this moves the issue away from being problem focused by bringing the focus to what's good. Any simple act of health gently reminds the dark side that the light is always there and can be taken in very small portions as needed. Spending time in nature is also so crucial to remind anyone with a drug habit that the beauty of nature is always there for them too, although they may need to continually immerse themselves in it for its healing to soak through; when one has deadened one's senses it does take time to re-awaken them. Bit by bit, that universal healing around and within us reminds us again and again of its existence, all we need to do is gently allow its presence in our lives, and drink it in, in however small doses we want at the time.

- It may be true that cutting down and effectively managing an addiction is as healing as quitting it entirely. Allowing yourself to manage it better builds your self-esteem and shows understanding to whatever it was that led you into addiction. People's self-worth can become so low, which is why I believe self-acceptance and compassion around the addiction—along with the suggestions above and a willingness to keep an addiction as a small or smaller portion of your day and week—may over time be a better cure than going cold turkey, as this may be too extreme for some addicts.

It's essential that people know they have the choice to completely release any addiction, yet in absence of doing so, pursuing healing is so important. It's not hypocritical to be an addict and seek healing (doing both good and bad), no matter what bad anyone does, working towards healing is always paramount.

Chapter 17 – Depression

- Do not be afraid to seek answers and to seek healing. We have access to so many healing methods. The idea of having a Reiki or a Tai Chi master; a kinesiologist or a counsellor (to name a few), is that you do not have to go through this alone! You can put yourself in the position to heal the pain with love and support, at your own pace, in your own time and on your own terms. You can start Tai Chi or Yoga classes (which are well known for their healing benefits) for as little as $10 a session, even less in some cases.

- We, as humans, have great ability to figure out our own solutions. It is time for us to become empowered with this ability, because no matter how terrible we think our problems are, they would only be compounded if we were living through a war. We must become empowered with our ability to solve our own problems simply because we can.

- People suffering from mental illness suffer even more under the mental health care system. Electric shock treatment *is* common, over prescription *is* common. There are many barbaric practices for our disabled and mentally

275

ill still in place (the treatment of people in some aged care facilities is also of great concern). My solution is to encourage all relevant institutions to implement essential growth fostering elements into their programs, such as good food, safe environment, creative activities, minimal drug prescription, counselling and lots of Eastern healing methods. Of course they would need funding and support from federal and state governments to do this. This would create a much saner world for all of us.

- Again, I highly recommend the book *You can heal your life* (Hay) for all those seeking healing. It explains methods of self-healing which you can do simply by *thinking* better, about yourself, and about everything. In many cases of depression, the power of the persons mind in bringing them down with difficult thoughts lacking in hope can become extreme. The mind *is* a powerful influence in our lives, and we must work towards its healing by refusing any inner dialogue that leaves us feeling we have nowhere to turn; as self-love is always a cure that exists within us.

Chapter 19 – More on society

- If you are feeling burnt out, tired, overworked, and stressed; if you feel any kind of lethargy or discontent; time in nature can be a powerful cure to help you re-energise, reinvigorate, and reconnect with your self. When we constantly have things on the go and are not doing any sort of replenishing, the simple acts of sitting by or hugging a tree; taking a walk in a park rich in greenery; splashing fresh water from a creek or river (or even the bathroom) on our faces; breathing deeply in the outdoors; and any other action that involves sharing in Mother Nature can truly be so wonderfully rejuvenating for mind, body and spirit. This can be easy to forget.

- Take the time to create even just 5 minutes a week where you sit in a quiet place of your home or any place where you can take some time out to relax, breathe, let go, unwind. Any form of relaxation or meditation is wonderful for strengthening yourself and brings you clarity which can greatly improve your state of mind.

- A very brief exercise of simply relaxing all areas of the face (using the method as shown in Ideas and Solutions, p. 119.) can show just how much tension we are holding and how much stress we need to release. There are a lot of meridian points on the face so this is an excellent exercise just on its own.

- Tune into everything that you feel is real, potent, natural, magical, and special to you. The more you allow yourself to indulge in and enjoy these energies the more you increase your capacity to accept and *embody* these qualities into your life.

PART THREE – Where do we go from here?

Chapter 22 – Global warming

- Be aware that every person *does* make a difference.
- Care about creating a positive difference in

everything you do.

- Watch Al Gore's *An Inconvenient Truth*. He may not be a saint, but I do believe he is doing some good here. The work of both David Suzuki and Peter Singer is also highly recommended.
- If we truly wanted a democratic Australia, it would be viable for a leader, such as John Howard, to run government alongside an Indigenous Elder. I can just imagine the conversations:

John Howard: 'Now, we got to sign this contract to expand our coal fire stations, and here's another one to continue mining uranium. So if you can just, ah, put your signature here … '
Elder: 'You cannot hurt the land.'

Howard: 'Oh well, but we have to, we've got investors, we've got buyers, we can't upset China, now let's not be hasty on this. Ah, what if I employ some of your people, get them on the projects?'

Elder: 'You cannot hurt the land.'